T0306488

EAT, SHARE, LOVE

About the Author

Kalpna Woolf is an award-winning food writer, entrepreneur and charity campaigner. Her love of food comes from her Indian heritage and from managing food TV series at the BBC with Nigella, Nigel Slater, Rick Stein and the Hairy Bikers. She brought her passion and expertise in spices and health into her first food book – Spice Yourself Slim – which is now in paperback as Spice Diet. She is well-known and highly respected on the food circuit as a festival chef, food writer, storyteller and seasoned food awards judge.

Kalpna's many achievements have been recognised by a clutch of national awards, including The Guild of Food Writers Inspiration Award, BBC's Food and Farming Food Hero Award, Crumbs Food Magazine Food Hero and the Asian Women of Achievement Award. She was also featured in Waitrose Magazine as one of "20 people Making the World a Better Place to Live and Eat in 2020".

Kalpna launched BeOnBoard – developing leaders from all backgrounds to step into decision-making roles to influence positive change for everyone – and in 2015 she founded her charity 91 Ways, which seeks to bring diverse communities together using the power of food to share stories and break down barriers.

Dedication

*Sharing our food and sharing our stories can build bridges.
I'd like to dedicate this book to people and communities
from all over the world who have a story to tell — I hope
this book will encourage you to share your most cherished
food memories and in this way bring greater
understanding and love to our world.*

EAT, SHARE, LOVE

©2022 91 Ways CIC, Kalpna Woolf &
Meze Publishing Limited

First edition printed in 2022 in the UK

ISBN: 978-1-910863-89-3

Created and compiled by: Kalpna Woolf

Edited by: Katie Fisher, Phil Turner

Designed by: Paul Cocker

Set Stylist: Kalpna Woolf

Props Stylist: Maria A. Perez

Project Manager: Hannah Boatfield

Photography by: Paul Gregory

Additional photography supplied by:
Jim Lampard, @JonCraig_Photos,
Rob Wicks @EatPictures, @RubyWalkerPhoto
@TimGreenPhoto

Publicity: Fiona Smith, Smith & Baxter

Meze sales, marketing & PR:
Emma Toogood, Lizzy Capps

Contributors: Katherine Dullforce, Lis Ellis,
Lizzie Morton

Printed and bound in the UK
by Bell & Bain Ltd, Glasgow

Published by Meze Publishing Limited
Unit 1b, 2 Kelham Square
Kelham Riverside
Sheffield S3 8SD
Web: www.mezepublishing.co.uk
Telephone: 0114 275 7709
Email: info@mezepublishing.co.uk

Contents

Sharing Our ... Snacks & Drinks

Sharing Our ... Sweets

Sharing Our ... Celebrations

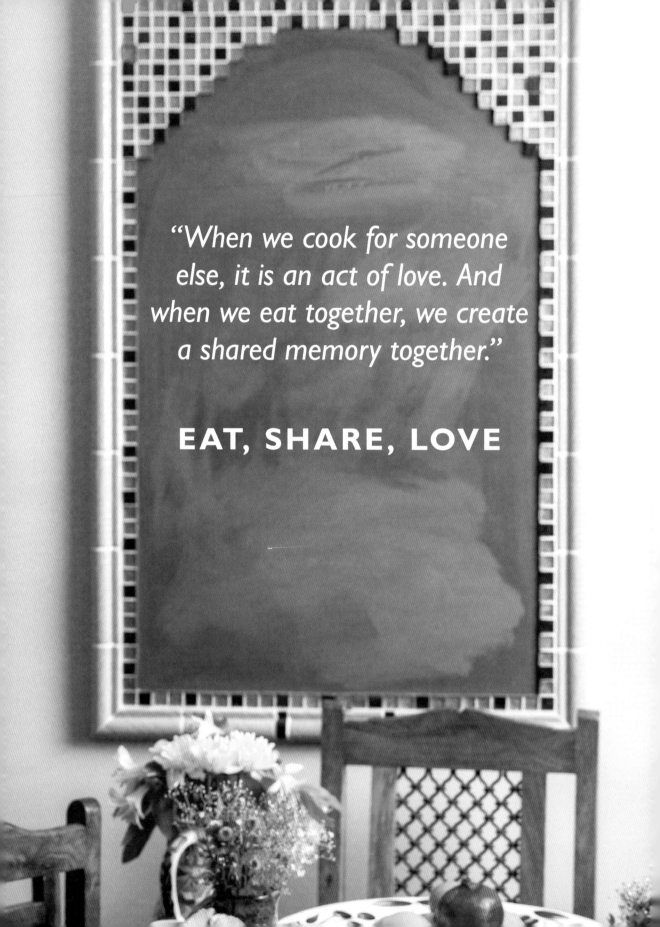

"When we cook for someone else, it is an act of love. And when we eat together, we create a shared memory together."

EAT, SHARE, LOVE

Introduction

Why does food mean so much to us? It's not just a primeval instinct for survival or even just the delicious sensory pleasure of tasting a beautifully made dish. It's more than that. When you stop and think about it, almost all of the favourite dishes we love have an important emotional connection or legacy for us and they are often bound up with our most important shared life experiences. Perhaps they're dishes we grew up with as children which were part of our daily family rituals; they might be meals we have enjoyed sharing and creating with our friends, partners and families; or they are intrinsically tied to our culture, traditions, religion or identity. So, our favourite foods are closely connected to who we are and with every treasured recipe there is a story and a memory attached – of love, friendship, happiness, loss, kindness, laughter and so much more. *Eat, Share, Love* is a collection of those intertwined recipes and stories: wonderfully enticing global dishes from ordinary cooks all over the UK alongside their compelling personal stories.

I grew up in an immigrant Hindu family in Southall in west London, where food was very much at the heart of our daily lives. Our food heritage was one of the most important things we had brought with us from India and it was a tradition we firmly held on to in this new country, even though initially as new communities started to form it wasn't always easy to find the ingredients we loved (spices and nuts were hard to find in Southall in the 1960s and my mother would routinely smuggle these into her suitcase on her trips to India). My father was at the heart of the fledgling community, helping other families to find much-needed work and housing, filling in application forms for them, and eventually founding the first Hindu temple in Southall. This meant that, as well as us five children, there were people dropping by our home all the time and they were nearly always asked to eat with us. So, for most of my childhood, myself, my mum and my three sisters were busily cooking in our tiny kitchen and the dining table was always supplied with bubbling pots of different dals and pulses, freshly cooked vegetables, rice and hot rotis. Even now, decades later, I can picture, smell and taste those dishes from my childhood. They are an inextricable part of me.

I still cook dal most weeks. I love the taste, the variety. It is healthy and nutritious, but I also cook it because at every step, I feel myself emotionally transported back to when my mum cooked it, from abating the hunger of five young children at a time when we had little money, to cheering me up when I felt down, comforting me when I was unwell or making me proud when I cooked it for my son and he said it was his favourite dish! It is also a dish steeped in our culture; dal has a place in our everyday life, at family events and is included proudly in our festive tables.

The dishes that my mum cooked then, all came from where she and my dad grew up in what is now Pakistan, and the history of those dishes goes back centuries further, to the influences of the Moghuls and earlier, from the time of Alexander the Great. The Moghuls occupied large parts of the country and India's art, music, poetry, food and language have been irrevocably inspired by them. Our family home had many ornate paintings of Moghul rulers hunting astride magnificent elephants or languishing in their opulent palaces and my father would relate vivid tales of how the Moghuls' kitchens were overseen by hundreds of chefs producing elaborate meals for daily consumption, and how their extravagant feasts would surpass those of anywhere in the world. Some of those dishes have made it into this book as they are very much part of my and my family's food journey: rich meat dishes such as Keema Kofte and my creamy Butter Chicken which I like to think was once served to emperors. These recipes are part of my Hindu heritage, but they also reflect a time when Hindus lived happily and peacefully cheek by jowl with their Muslim neighbours, went to school together, worked together and often feasted together.

Like most of us, my culinary horizons have broadened immeasurably over the years as I have accumulated new food memories, from exploring the delights of elaborate French cuisine at university to being inspired by global travels, which introduced me to captivating new dishes from places like Italy and Vietnam. Marrying into new cultures led to discovering new foods and traditions too, as did a long career working at the BBC, where I had the luck to end up overseeing all of the BBC's television cookery series and seeing first-hand the dishes created by the likes of Nigella, The Hairy Bikers, Lorraine Pascale and many others. Now I find that I am handing over this wealth of culinary influences, stories and inheritance dishes to the next generation, talking recipes and cooking techniques with my son Ben who has become a passionate and talented cook in his own right.

I have always known that food – and the stories behind what we eat and why – has a power to connect us and that food can be a universal language. When I decided to leave the BBC after 25 years and was working out what to do next, I knew instinctively that food and helping and supporting under-represented diverse communities were going to be part of my future somehow. By chance, I then stumbled across a Census statistic for my home city of Bristol which showed that there were 91 different languages spoken in the city. I was really surprised by this, by how little I knew about all these myriad language communities and how unconnected the city felt at that time. I wondered what I could do to help and whether food might be the key to unlocking those connections.

So, six years ago I founded a charity called **91 Ways to Build A Global City** (www.91ways.org) with the aim of bringing communities together to build greater understanding between people from different backgrounds. I started with a launch event in 2015 inviting communities from all over Bristol to bring and share their food. The event was a huge success, attracting hundreds of people from all sorts of backgrounds. A spark was lit, the foodie city enthusiastically embraced the idea and over the next few years the charity grew and grew. We run community events, teach children from disadvantaged backgrounds about food in local schools and lonely elder members of communities how to cook together, help to provide food for the city's thousands of disadvantaged families and run dozens of events in marginalised communities in and around the city, including regular supper clubs hosted by community cooks from all over the world. At the heart of the charity's trademark supper club events are ordinary home cooks from different communities, showcasing their favourite dishes and explaining how and why they came to cook them. The combination of often unfamiliar dishes and captivating personal stories is nearly always mesmerising for everyone who attends the suppers, whatever their own background. The suppers not only give guests the chance to try new dishes but also introduce them to cultures and communities they often know very little about, and all sorts of surprising friendships and connections are made.

Those 91 Ways meals and stories – and my own food journey – have very much been the inspiration for this book. Some of the supper club cooks are featured here and all the proceeds from the sale of this book will go towards allowing us to continue our work with 91 Ways.

Eat, Share, Love is a book which very much reflects the UK's myriad cultures and cuisines, many of which are not often represented. Every recipe in this book has its own story to tell, as individually surprising and different as the dishes themselves, either enticing us to try new recipes for the first time or giving fresh meaning to foods we know and love. It's very much a collection of mini-memoirs, of recipes and stories handed down through family generations past and present. Its dishes range from a ruby-red Russian beetroot salad to a luscious Sudanese aubergine stew and a Bristolian take on the enduring English favourite, prawn cocktail. Its heart-warming stories include the tale of love and romance behind Moh's Persian ghormeh sabzi – a mouth-watering lamb stew with dried limes and beans – and Beth's childhood memories of her grandmother's silver sugar shaker which was an unforgettable part of her rhubarb crumble. Baljeet shares an evocative memory of the food made at the Indian festival of Holi, when her mum cooked delicious sweet pancakes (malpura), while Lucio relates a heart-rending story about the favourite family dish (carne de panela) his mother used to cook and how he made it for her when she was seriously ill and too frail to cook it herself.

I'd like to think that the joy of this book is in reminding ourselves just how much our favourite foods actually mean to us, and that by the simple act of sharing our food and stories we can make unexpected connections with each other which can bridge our cultural, religious and ethnic divides and bring us all closer together.

All the proceeds from this book will go to the 91 Ways charity. You can donate to us, volunteer with us, or learn more about our work by visiting our website, 91ways.org.

SHARING OUR ...
LIGHT EATS

"My favourite Jewish holiday in childhood was Passover: I loved the ceremony, the songs, the story, and the celebration with family... Truth be told, the biggest delight of the evening was not any food tied to the Passover story, but the morsels that came in the starter before the main meal." – Rabbi Monique Mayer

When my father first came to this country, he shared a room in a house with other Indian men who, like him, had come to earn enough money to bring their families over to this country. This dish reminds me of the sacrifices my father and so many people like him made, leaving all their families behind and making the long journeys to a strange land.

Although the men were mainly well educated, the only jobs they could get were hard, manual factory jobs. In fact, the conditions were backbreaking, with the Indian workers often given the worst jobs, paid less than their white colleagues and routinely given the worst shifts. The men would rent rooms together in one house to save money, many working two or three jobs in one day, but once a day, they would try to cook together.

At that time, you couldn't get many of the spices or Indian produce which are now readily available. So, many dishes were invented to resemble the dishes which had been eaten back home. One of these was what we call Indian baked beans, very loosely based on our Rajma sabzi which is a kidney bean curry. My father remembered buying tinned baked beans, but finding them very sweet, so they improvised by adding the usual base for curries – onions, tomatoes and some spices – and this became the dish the men would cook up when they were tired after working night shifts in the factories. It was filling and cheap. My father passed away over 30 years ago, but we still cook Indian Baked Beans for brunch in our family and I love cooking this at 91 Ways events for our communities. It is nourishing, tasty and has been adopted by the 91 Ways team as our 'Jazzy Beans'.

MY FATHER'S INDIAN BAKED BEANS

Preparation time: 10 minutes • Cooking time: 15 minutes • Serves 4

100g butter • 5-6 spring onions, roughly chopped including the green tops • Small handful of fresh coriander, stems roughly chopped and leaves finely chopped • ½ tsp red chilli flakes or 1 fresh red chilli, finely chopped (or more to taste) • ½ tsp ground turmeric • 1 tsp ground coriander • 3 medium fresh tomatoes or 8 cherry tomatoes, roughly chopped • 2 x 400g tins of baked beans • 4 free-range eggs (optional) • Salt and pepper

Heat the butter in a medium skillet on a medium heat. Add the chopped spring onions and coriander stems and cook until soft. Mix in the chilli, turmeric and ground coriander. Cook for 1 to 2 minutes and then add the fresh tomatoes. Cook on a medium heat until the tomatoes melt down (around 3 to 4 minutes). Pour in the baked beans and leave to gently cook for 5 minutes. Crack in the eggs, if using, and continue to cook for 3 minutes until the eggs are done. Season with salt and pepper to taste, then scatter fresh coriander leaves over the dish and serve simply with crusty bread.

KIRI HODI AND GRANDMA PERERA'S PAPPADUM CURRY

Preparation time: 10 minutes • Cooking time: 30 minutes • Serves 4

2 tbsp vegetable oil • I small cinnamon stick • I tsp fenugreek seeds • 2-4 green chillies, chopped (adjust according to taste) • 10 curry leaves (can be substituted with 2 bay leaves) • I rampe (pandan) leaf (optional) • I-2 red onions, sliced • 3-4 cloves of garlic, sliced • I tsp ground turmeric • 50g coconut cream • 400ml hot water • Lime juice and salt, to taste

Heat the vegetable oil in a saucepan over a medium heat. First, stir in the cinnamon stick and fenugreek seeds. After a minute or so, add the chillies, curry leaves and rampe, if using. Mix well, then stir in the onion and garlic. Sauté over a low heat until soft.

Add the turmeric and mix well. Dissolve the coconut cream in the hot water and pour it into the pan. Stir and bring to the boil, then turn the heat down and simmer for about 5 minutes.

Turn off the heat and add lime juice and salt to taste.

If you want to make curries for lunch using kiri hodi, choose one or two of the following to compliment your other dishes and serve with rice.

For a green bean curry, top and tail then halve 225g of green beans. Parboil them before stirring in after the onions and garlic. Simmer for about 10 minutes.

For a potato curry, peel and cube 450g of potatoes. Parboil them before stirring in after the onions and garlic. Simmer for about 10 minutes.

For a fish curry, cut 600g of cod or salmon into chunks. Fry them lightly in a separate pan, then add them to the curry when the sauce is simmering for the last 10 minutes until the fish is cooked.

For my grandma's secret pappadum curry, add some broken up fried pappadums (I cheat here and buy ready-made pappadums from the supermarket) to the kiri hodi and serve immediately.

Everyone in Sri Lanka knows kiri hodi (white curry) with string hoppers* and coconut sambal as a breakfast dish. It is mild and creamy, which suits most people's tastes, including young children.

However, kiri hodi is quite versatile and can be used as a base to make a fish curry, a green bean curry or a potato curry for lunch too.

Personally, I think nothing beats my grandma's pappadum curry. Whenever we visited our grandparents for a rice and curry lunch, she transformed kiri hodi into a magical dish simply by adding some fried pappadums broken into small pieces. I have never forgotten this taste so it must have some magic attached to it! No one else ever cooked it. We thought she was very clever and the best cook in the world!

*String hoppers, also known as idiyappam, are made from roasted rice flour dough which is pressed through a string mould into noodles and then steamed. They can be substituted with vermicelli.

SANA ELGORAISH

SANA'S FRESH FETA AND AUBERGINE SALAD

This is a favourite dish because the combination of ingredients is delicious and a great balance between healthy and unhealthy. I've prepared this for my friends and family who said it's one of the best aubergine salads they've ever tasted! I also made this for the 91 Ways Peace Feast.

Preparation time: 20 minutes • Cooking time: 10 minutes • Serves 4 as a side or 2 as a main

2 carrots • 2 small or medium aubergines • ½ a red, orange and yellow pepper • 8-10 tbsp sunflower oil • 1 packet of feta cheese • 3 cloves of garlic, peeled and crushed • Small handful of fresh coriander leaves • 3 tbsp yoghurt • 2 tsp apple cider vinegar • 2 tsp ground coriander • 1 tsp peanut butter • 1 tsp salt • 1 tsp pepper • ½ a lemon, juiced • ½ a pomegranate

Cut the carrots, aubergines and peppers into small cubes. Heat up the oil in a wide pan and fry the diced carrot for 3 minutes, then remove it and fry the aubergine until golden brown. Remove from the pan and leave it to cool down.

Mix the fried carrot and aubergine with the fresh peppers, crumbled feta cheese, crushed garlic and fresh coriander in a large serving bowl. For the dressing, mix the yoghurt with the vinegar, ground coriander, peanut butter, salt, pepper and lemon juice in a separate smaller bowl or jug. Pour the dressing over the salad and finish by sprinkling it with pomegranate seeds just before serving.

KALPNA WOOLF

I close my eyes and imagine the weekday dinner table at our family home: a fresh tablecloth hand-embroidered by my mum, a bowl of steaming tempered dal, soft white rotis wrapped in a warm cloth, and always a plate of gorgeous vegetables, magically spiced and perfectly complementing the creamy yoghurt set overnight in our warm airing cupboard! Picturing this, my heart swells with joy.

These are two of my favourite vegetable dishes: crispy aubergine slices, spiced with a citrusy tang from dried mango powder and adorned with shiny red pomegranate seeds and yoghurt, simple to make but surprisingly delicious. The second is an easy and quick way of making a Punjabi classic: gobi, aloo and mutter (cauliflower, potatoes and peas) in an oven tray. I hope you enjoy them.

Photo: Rob Wicks @EatPictures

CRISPY AMCHOOR AUBERGINE

Preparation time: 15 minutes • Cooking time: 30 minutes • Serves 4

2 medium aubergines • 3 tbsp ground turmeric • 2 tbsp ground coriander • 1 tbsp red chilli powder • 1 tbsp amchoor powder (dried mango powder) • 1 tsp salt • Oil for frying • 150g natural yoghurt • 50g fresh pomegranate seeds • A small handful of fresh coriander leaves, to garnish

Turn the grill onto its highest setting. Slice the aubergine into 1cm rounds. Gently score each slice without cutting all the way through the aubergine. Combine all the spices and salt in a shallow bowl, then coat each slice of aubergine in the spice mix on both sides.

Pour enough oil into a frying pan to cover the bottom with a thin layer and bring to a high heat. Start to add the spiced aubergine to the pan but don't overcrowd it. Quickly brown the slices on both sides and then transfer them to a baking sheet lined with parchment paper. Repeat until all done.

Place the baking sheet under the hot grill and cook until crispy. Garnish the aubergine with dollops of yoghurt, pomegranate seeds and coriander leaves. Eat with bread or salad, or with dal and rice.

QUICK ROASTED GOBI, ALOO AND MUTTER

Preparation time: 20 minutes • Cooking time: 35 minutes • Serves 4

8-10 tbsp olive oil • 2 tbsp cumin seeds • 2 large potatoes, peeled and diced into 2.5cm cubes • 5cm fresh ginger, grated • 1 small cauliflower, chopped into florets (keep the outer leaves) • ½ tbsp ground turmeric • ½ tbsp ground coriander • ½ tsp ground cumin • ½ tsp red chilli powder (or to taste) • ½ tsp salt • 8-10 cherry tomatoes, quartered • Handful of frozen peas • Large handful of fresh coriander leaves and stalks

Preheat the oven to 180°c and heat up the oil in a roasting tin. When hot, sprinkle in the cumin seeds. When they sizzle, add the cubed potatoes and grated ginger. Mix well and then place in the hot oven for 10 minutes.

Now add the cauliflower florets. Return the tin to the oven for 10 to 12 minutes. After this time, the cauliflower and potatoes should be almost cooked. Add the cauliflower leaves, spices and salt. Mix well and place back in the oven for 5 minutes.

Mix in the fresh tomatoes and frozen peas. Cook for a final 5 to 7 minutes in the oven, after which time the cauliflower and potatoes should be soft. Chop the fresh coriander and sprinkle over the roasted vegetables, then serve with roti or bread or as an accompaniment to anything!

This is my mother's recipe for her yummy salmon patties, which was passed down to me many years ago. As children, it was always our favourite weekend lunch; my sister and I, and my father too, could never have enough of them, particularly when they were served with our favourite homemade chips. Not good for the waistline, but that was not our concern back then: it was always about how many we could fit on our plate!

Cosy family mealtimes, chatter round the table, memories of Mum by the stove wearing her blue fish hat and pinnie as she fried the patties to perfection… We loved them most when they were hot off the pan, but equally were happy to eat them cold, should there be any leftovers!

I have since passed the recipe on to my own family and know without a doubt that it will be passed down the generations.

GRANDMA LIVINGSTONE'S SALMON PATTIES

Preparation time: 15 minutes plus 30 minutes for resting • Cooking time: 20 minutes • Makes 10-12 patties or 20 cocktail party bites

3 large eggs • 480g tinned salmon (if preferred, use the same quantity of fresh salmon, cooked and flaked) • ½ small onion, grated • 1 tsp lemon zest • ½ tsp salt • Ground black pepper • 4 tbsp medium matzo meal • Handful of fine dried breadcrumbs • Oil, for frying • Lemon wedges, to serve

To begin, beat the eggs together in a large bowl. Drain the tinned salmon, flake it up and remove any bones. Add the flaked salmon to the eggs along with the grated onion, lemon zest, salt and a fairly generous amount of black pepper, then mix in the medium matzo meal.

The mixture should now be just firm enough to form into patties. With wet hands, form the salmon mixture into patties or balls as preferred and then coat these in the fine breadcrumbs.

Leave the patties to rest for 30 minutes. Fry the patties in hot oil on both sides until brown. Serve warm or at room temperature with lemon wedges and homemade chips if you can!

Photo: John Wildgoose

In the early 1950s my mother travelled around Italy for several months. How extraordinary that must have seemed to a young woman fresh from university, with memories of the war still vivid and raw. I wish now that I had talked to her more about her experience. I assume that she went for the art, but I know that the food made a lasting impact on her. How could it not, after a decade of rationing? Among the many Italian dishes she cooked for our family as I was growing up, two stand out above the rest: grilled pepper salads and baked fennel drenched with butter and parmesan. I still adore them both and think of my mother with gratitude and love as I slide the baking dish into the oven, even more so as I sit down to eat.

IL FINOCCHIO AL FORNO DI MIA MAMMA
(MY MOTHER'S BAKED FENNEL)

You don't really need a proper recipe for this; just be enthusiastic with the butter and cheese.

Preparation time: 10 minutes • Cooking time: 30-35 minutes • Serves any number

Fennel bulbs • Butter • Salt and pepper • Freshly grated parmesan

Preheat the oven to 200°c (180°c fan or Gas Mark 6). Trim the fennel, slicing off the fibrous ends. Cut the bulbs into wedges: 4 if they are relatively small, 8 or more if large.

Cook the fennel in a pan of salted boiling water until tender (around 5 minutes) and then drain it really, really, really thoroughly. Press down gently on the tender fennel with your hands to get rid of any water trapped in the layers.

Butter an ovenproof dish generously. Lay the fennel in the dish, no more than a couple of layers thick. Season with pepper, dot generously with butter then dredge with a blanket of parmesan.

Bake the fennel in the preheated oven for 20 to 25 minutes until the cheese has browned and the butter is sizzling cheerfully. Let it cool for a few minutes, then serve with wedges of bread to mop up the buttery juices.

Bhorta is a particular type of Bengali food which is basically mashed vegetables, fish or seafood mixed with chopped onions and herbs. There are a number of traditional bhortas we grew up eating here in the UK and I have many memories from childhood of my mum making various types of bhortas, sometimes with traditional ingredients and other times with adapted ingredients to take account of what was available here locally. Aubergine (brinjal), prawn (chingri), potato (aloo), fish (mach) and bean (green or tinned) bhortas were all regular family favourites. One of my brothers loved aloo bhorta so much he would request it every day!

Though many bhortas are made with raw onions, some can be made with cooked onions or more usually with shallots, red onions or spring onions as they are milder. Some people use green chillies and others use dried red chillies.

When we were little and fewer 'Asian' ingredients were readily available in the shops here in Bristol, I remember my mum would fry herrings (oily fish) and then pick out all the bones, very finely chop fresh mustard leaves grown in our back garden with seeds brought from Bangladesh, and then mix these ingredients with finely sliced onions, a little bit of fresh ginger and chopped green chillies to create the traditional mach (fish) bhorta eaten all over Bangladesh.

Mach bhorta was a task that used to take quite a while for my mother to make; even now I can't slice my onions as finely. Though she was used to using a kitchen knife, she would occasionally use the dha or boti, a traditional chopping instrument from Bangladesh, Bengal and Nepal used to cut vegetables and fish while sitting on the ground (which I have never dared to use).

When smoked peppered mackerel became readily available in the shops and supermarkets here it became a quick and easy substitute for the fried fish. For my mother it became a delight to make bhorta using smoked mackerel as it came pre-cooked and deboned, especially as her health deteriorated, and it's still a family favourite even among the next (third) generation. I regularly make smoked mackerel bhorta but substitute the fresh mustard leaves with either chopped watercress or spring onions.

SMOKED PEPPERED MACKEREL BHORTA

This is an incredibly quick and simple recipe for a comforting meal with rice, especially after a long work day.

Preparation time: 5 minutes • Serves 4

1 pack of smoked peppered mackerel • 1 small red onion, finely chopped • 100g watercress, roughly chopped • 2-3 spring onions, finely chopped • Sprinkle of red chilli flakes or 2 green chillies, finely chopped

Mash the smoked mackerel in a bowl and mix in all the ingredients. Stir well and garnish with the chilli flakes or chopped green chilli. Smoked peppered mackerel is the preferred choice but you can use plain smoked mackerel or tinned mackerel fillets, just remember to add additional chilli flakes or finely chopped green chillies to taste.

When Kalpna first came to me with the idea for 91 Ways, back in 2014, little did we know that it would lead us to this page in a book of 91 recipes from across the world. Our first conversation began with the question, "what is your earliest food memory?" and I was magically transported back into my childhood kitchen, cooking with Nona. I could smell the chicken soup bubbling on the hob, feel her hand gently guiding mine as she taught me to squash and then peel the cloves of garlic.

I was born in London, but my spiritual home is Argentina. The food we shared and the stories I overheard have stayed with me long beyond her lifetime. It was brutal trying to choose one recipe to share, but this one transcends all others, quite simply because it literally goes with anything. Spicing up a soup; transforming a sauce; smeared generously on a slab of steak, fresh off the asado; or simply dig in with some fresh bread. It's great with halloumi and tofu as well.

You can mix it up depending on how you feel on the day. Dial up the chilli, add some lime instead of lemon juice, or experiment with different herbs. Here's how we like it.

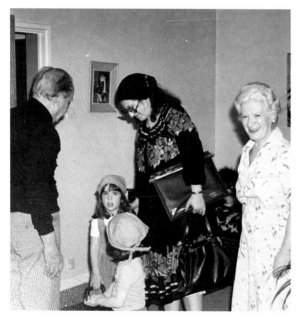

ARGENTINIAN CHIMICHURRI

Preparation time: 25 minutes • Makes enough for 4 dishes

2 bunches of fresh flat leaf parsley • 2 sprigs of thyme • 6 cloves of garlic • 1 fresh chilli • ½ a red onion or 3 spring onions • 1 lemon, juiced • 2 tbsp cider vinegar • 2 tbsp olive oil • Salt and freshly ground black pepper, to taste

Remove the stems from the parsley and thyme so you are left with just the leaves, then finely chop them. Crush the garlic, deseed the chilli and finely chop the onion. Stir all the ingredients together, check and adjust the flavours to suit your tastes, and serve however you like.

MY GRANDMA'S KURDISH KUFTE SOUP

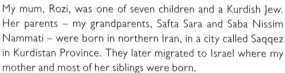

My mum, Rozi, was one of seven children and a Kurdish Jew. Her parents – my grandparents, Safta Sara and Saba Nissim Nammati – were born in northern Iran, in a city called Saqqez in Kurdistan Province. They later migrated to Israel where my mother and most of her siblings were born.

I adored visiting my grandma (safta) in Israel and have such wonderful memories of playing in her garden. The smells and colours that would come from the garden and her small kitchen were sensational and will stick in my memory forever. I loved being surrounded by my warm, loving Israeli family who provided unconditional love.

My safta had various fruit trees that she grew herself. We adored eating fresh pomegranates off her pomegranate tree and as toddlers she would feed us the pomegranate seeds. Chickens and ducks ran around alongside wild tortoises and the scent of fresh basil or lime leaves from the trees would waft through the hot air. Safta Sara was self-sufficient, growing lots of vegetables and fruits as well as sewing her children's clothing. She was an extremely shy, modest person and a true inspiration.

Uncle Meir married a wonderful Jewish woman, also called Rozi, whose roots are Turkish. Safta Sara taught Rozi how to cook delicious Kurdish dishes before marrying Meir and so the recipe for her kufte soup got passed on to my aunty. She made it every Friday night without fail when we stayed with them. The smell of bone broth radiated through her home and I loved drinking it, even though it was boiling hot outside. We demolished this dish! My aunty Rozi taught me how to make kufte soup and I now make it at home in Bristol, with my own twist.

I think that's how recipes work; the knowledge gets passed on through the generations. I have my beautiful mother to thank for allowing me to cook alongside her in the kitchen. I thank my mother for opening my eyes to her incredible, colourful, loving, heritage in the land of Israel. I would not be the person I am today without these experiences and memories that will be embodied in me for the rest of my life. Thank you ema, the best mother in the world.

Rozi kindly passed the family recipe to me, and I am so happy to pass this nourishing recipe onto you. So, as my aunty and most Israelis would say before eating, beteavon (enjoy your meal)! Food unites us which is the greatest gift of all.

NATASHA ORSON

MY GRANDMA'S KURDISH KUFTE SOUP

Preparation time: 30 minutes • Cooking time: up to 6 hours • Serves 8-10

For the kufte balls • 1kg minced beef • 500g minced chicken • 100g uncooked rice • 100g uncooked bulgur wheat
• 1 bunch of fresh parsley, finely chopped • 1 tsp hawaij (a Yemeni spice blend used in soups) • 1 tsp ground turmeric
• ½ tsp ground cinnamon • Salt and pepper, to taste

For the soup • 1 large chicken carcass (around 4-5kg) • 3 big pieces of beef bone marrow • 1 tsp ground turmeric
• 1 tsp hawaij • Salt, to taste • 6-7 large carrots, cut into large chunks

For the kufte balls

Combine all the ingredients in a bowl and mix well. Roll the kufte mixture into medium-size balls, bearing in mind that they will expand during cooking as they have rice and bulgur wheat inside them. Set the kufte aside while you prepare the soup broth.

For the soup

Put the chicken carcass and the beef bone marrow in a large pan and fill it with cold water. Bring this to the boil and cook on a high heat for 30 minutes. Keep skimming and scooping out any dirt or fat that appears on the surface of the liquid. After 30 minutes, reduce the heat to a very low simmer.

Once the bone broth seems clean and clear, add the turmeric, hawaij and salt. Gently drop in the kufte balls and carrots, then cook at a very low simmer for 5 hours.

To serve the soup, remove the chicken carcass and bones, then ladle the broth into bowls and share out the carrot chunks and kufte balls.

RUSSIAN BEETROOT SALAD (VINEGRET)

When I was growing up, my mum always cooked this as a healthy go-to dish to keep in the fridge. It is fresh, nutritious, full of goodness and something I regularly make at home, especially since I cooked it for the 91 Ways International Peace Café, which reminded me how much I love it!

Preparation time: 10 minutes • Cooking time: 20 minutes • Serves 4

3-4 new potatoes • 2 medium carrots • 4 medium beetroot • 4-5 medium gherkins or 3-4 tbsp sauerkraut • 1 banana shallot • 1 small tin of peas (or boiled fresh peas) • Sunflower oil, to dress • Salt and pepper

Boil the potatoes, carrots and beetroot in their skins until they are cooked through. Cook the beetroot in a separate pan to avoid colouring the other vegetables. Once cooked, transfer the vegetables onto a paper towel to drain and let them cool. Once you can handle them, peel the skins off the cooked vegetables and cube them.

Dice the gherkins and finely chop the shallot. Place the beetroot into a bowl and thoroughly coat it with sunflower oil; this will stop the colour from leaking into the rest of the ingredients. Mix all the ingredients together in a serving bowl, including the peas and sauerkraut if using, then add salt and pepper to taste. Serve the salad with bread alongside.

VOLGAN BORSCHT

Borscht reminds me of being reunited with friends and family, because it is the first thing my mum cooks when I return to Russia. Now I share it with my family and friends in Bristol too!

Preparation time: 15 minutes • Cooking time: up to 4 hours • Serves 4

3 medium carrots • 3 medium onions • 1 shin of beef, bone in • 2 tsp salt • ½ tsp pepper • 3 bay leaves • 2 medium beetroot • ½ lemon, juiced • 1 tbsp vegetable oil • 2 tbsp tomato purée • 2 medium potatoes (preferably waxy) • ¼ small white cabbage • Small bunch of fresh dill

Roughly chop one carrot, peel an onion and place them in a large pan with the beef shin, salt and 3.5 litres of water on a medium heat. Just before the liquid reaches boiling point, add the pepper and bay leaves, then turn down the heat and simmer for 3 to 4 hours until the meat is tender and falls off the bone. Keep skimming the scum from the top of the pan as it appears. Once cooked, remove the beef from the pan and shred the meat into chunks. Keep the stock but discard the veg.

Meanwhile, julienne the beetroot and remaining carrots. Place the beetroot in a pan with a tablespoon of water and fresh lemon juice. Cover and simmer until soft. Dice the remaining onions. Put the oil, julienned carrot and diced onion into a frying pan and gently sweat on a medium heat. Once soft, add the tomato purée and a little water to loosen it. Cook for a few minutes, stirring regularly.

Strain the beef stock into a clean pan. Cut the potatoes into bite-size pieces and add them to the stock, bring to the boil and cook for 5 minutes. Shred the cabbage, add it to the pan and leave to simmer until cooked. Stir all the other cooked vegetables into the stock and bring back to the boil. Finely chop and then add the dill. Allow the flavours to infuse for 5 minutes then serve with the beef.

PATRICIA ALVAREZ

My mum had a small stall in a market in Chile but her dream was to have a shop, so I have done that here in Bristol with La Ruca. I have a café upstairs with a photo of me and my mum, to remember that it was always her dream. I often cooked the dish that I am sharing here for my customers and they loved it. It's something that we always ate in Chile in the summertime and was always fulfilling; we didn't need any more food than that and it was the best we had. It always reminds me of home.

This is a recipe that I modified from what is called porotos granados in Chile, which is made with fresh pinto beans (which are not easily found in England) and very big round yellow pumpkins. 'Porotos a la Chacarera' can be translated as 'bean from the countryside' where the maize is grown. This dish is eaten with plenty of fresh basil in the central part of Chile in the summertime.

POROTOS A LA CHACARERA

Preparation time: 8 hours • Cooking time: 1 hour 30 minutes • Serves 6

500g dried pinto beans • 2 tbsp olive oil • 1 large onion • 1 red pepper • 2-3 cloves of garlic • 3 tsp smoked paprika • 1 tsp chilli powder • 1 tsp oregano • 2 courgettes • 2 sweet potatoes • 2 tins of sweetcorn • 1 bunch of fresh basil • Splash of milk or water • Flour to thicken, if needed • Salt, to taste

Soak the pinto beans overnight, then rinse and cook them for about 1 hour, until soft to the touch with not too much water left in the pan.

Heat the olive oil in a frying pan while you dice the onion and pepper, then chop the garlic. Add them to the heated oil along with the paprika, chilli powder and oregano. Fry until the onions are soft. Meanwhile, chop the courgettes and sweet potatoes into bite-size chunks, then drain the corn.

Add the spiced onion mixture to the cooked beans along with the prepared vegetables and 1 tin of sweetcorn. Let it cook all together on a low heat until the vegetables are cooked. The stew must not be too watery.

In a bowl, combine the remaining tin of corn with the fresh basil and a splash of milk or water. Mash or whisk until it is all mixed into a paste consistency. If it is too runny add a little maize flour or semolina (any other type of flour will work too) and stir in to thicken.

When the stew is ready, stir in the sweetcorn and basil paste to give the stew a nice thick texture. Season to taste with salt. This can now be served as it is, or you can add grated cheese, a pinch of smoked paprika and chopped fresh basil to finish. Just use vegan cheese to make it vegan!

Our mum was a wonderful cook. She could take a simple vegetable and transform it into a delicious and nourishing meal for us. I'd watch her patiently cutting the courgettes, stirring them into the pan and creating a surprisingly tasty dish from everyday ingredients. She loved to cook and, as she grew older, I wanted to look after her so I would tentatively make the dishes she liked. Our mum enjoyed this sabzi but she would comment something like: "hmm, don't you know how to cook?" with a cheeky smile. Of course, this was all in jest as she tucked into her food. I know she loved eating this. I miss her deeply. Here is the recipe, with love.

MY MUM'S TORIYAN KI SABZI
(COURGETTE SABZI)

Preparation time: 10 minutes • Cooking time: 25 minutes
• Serves 4

**6 spring onions, chopped (including the green stems)
• 2 large beef tomatoes, roughly chopped • 2.5cm (1 inch)
fresh ginger, peeled and grated • 6-8 tbsp olive oil
• ½ tbsp ground turmeric • ½ tsp ground coriander
• ½ tsp chilli flakes • Salt, to taste • 3 large courgettes,
peeled and diced • 30g butter • Fresh coriander leaves,
finely chopped**

Combine the spring onions, tomatoes and ginger in a small blender and blend to a smooth pulp. Heat the olive oil in a large frying pan and when hot, pour in the tomato mixture. Reduce the heat to low, cook for 10 minutes and then stir in the spices and salt. Add the diced courgette and cook for 15 to 20 minutes until soft.

Serve this sabzi with the butter melting on top, sprinkled with the fresh coriander. We would eat this with chapati or pita bread, though my mum liked to eat it on soft, warm, buttered toast. At home, we would have it with rice and dal.

GARLIC BHINDI (OKRA) STIR FRY

On her first visit from Pakistan, my mother taught me this dish. As I watched her confidently cook, I remembered visiting vegetable markets with her as a child, and now I'm teaching my own daughter this simple recipe! If you like, add 4 tablespoons of natural yoghurt to the marinade which makes the bhindi softer. This variation may take a few extra minutes to cook.

Preparation time: 20 minutes, plus 30 minutes marinating • Cooking time: 25 minutes • Serves 4

500g bhindi (okra) • 4-5 green chillies, chopped • I tsp crushed red chillies • I tsp ground turmeric • I tsp cumin seeds • ¾ tsp red chilli powder • ¾ tsp kalongi (nigella seeds) • I tsp salt • 3-4 tbsp oil, for frying • I bulb of garlic, cloves peeled and finely sliced (use less if preferred) • Small bunch of fresh coriander leaves, washed and chopped (optional)

Wash and then thoroughly dry the bhindi with a tea towel. Top and tail each bhindi, then make a lengthways slit without completely halving it and cut into 3 pieces. If your bhindi is over-ripened, some seeds may be tough so discard any larger bead-like seeds from the top end. No harm done if you want to leave them in though.

Add all the spices, nigella seeds and salt to the prepared bhindi and mix well. Heat a little oil in a large pan and lightly fry the sliced garlic until very light brown, then remove it from the pan and add to the bhindi mixture. Leave this to marinate for at least 30 minutes, or it can be prepared a few hours in advance and left to one side covered with a tea towel (my mum likes to keep it in the sun for an hour).

Heat the remaining oil in the same pan used for garlic and bring it to a high heat, then add marinated bhindi and stir quickly for a few minutes. Turn the heat down to medium while stirring gently so as not to break up the pieces. This is an important step as it stops the bhindi becoming gooey and sticky. Keep stirring with a spatula or a wooden spoon until everything is coated with oil. This usually takes about 10 to 12 minutes.

Reduce the heat further and cover the pan with a lid to let the bhindi cook slowly for another 10 minutes. Test it for softness and spices at this stage and adjust accordingly. When done, stir in the chopped coriander while the bhindi is still hot. I love serving this dish with freshly made chapatis and a simple raita, but toasted naan bread works just as well!

Food is very much linked to our heritage, and many of my most favourite recipes take me back to my childhood, with family cooking in the grandparents' old kitchen. My grandparents lived in a small village in Moldova, and my grandmother was a Food Tech teacher at the local school. Nobody cooked like she cooked, and this passion for food was passed on to her three daughters, then to her grandchildren. I baked my first cake at the age of seven and have been cooking ever since.

This particular recipe for dumplings stuffed with feta cheese takes me back to the grandparents' old kitchen. They had a new kitchen in the new house, but somehow when we all gathered around at holidays we'd all cram together in the old tiny kitchen. You could barely move in it, but it had the best atmosphere, chat and laughter. The dumplings take time to make by hand, but there is no better activity for a family or group of friends. I love making them with my children. Although my family is now thousands of miles away, when we gather in the kitchen to make them it feels like I am that kid in my grandparents' kitchen again.

MOLDOVAN DUMPLINGS
(COLȚUNAȘI CU BRÂNZĂ)

Preparation time: 40 minutes • Cooking time: 10 minutes • Makes 30-35

For the filling • 500g feta cheese and ricotta • 2 eggs

For the dough • 500g flour • 1 egg • 1 tsp salt • 3 tbsp oil • 200ml lukewarm water

To serve • Knob of butter • Sour cream or yoghurt

First, make the filling by crumbling the feta and ricotta into a bowl and mixing in the eggs. Next, make the dough by placing the flour in a large bowl or on a work surface and making a well in the centre. Break the egg into it, then add the salt, oil and lukewarm water a little at a time. Bring the dough together, kneading well and adding more flour or water as necessary to form a smooth ball. Divide the dough in half and cover both pieces with a bowl or towel. Let it rest for 20 minutes.

Now it's time to assemble the dumplings on a floured work surface. Roll out the first half of the dough to about 3mm thick (1/8 inch) and press out circles with a 5cm (2 inch) round cutter or glass. Spoon one and a half teaspoons of the filling into the middle of each circle. Fold them in half and pinch the edges together tightly so that the filling is sealed in. Gather up the scraps, re-roll them and keep filling the circles until you run out of dough.

Bring a large pot of water to the boil, adding salt and a few drops of oil. Put the dumplings into the water and let them boil for 3 to 5 minutes until they rise to the surface. Drain and serve hot. The best way to serve these is by adding a dollop of butter to the hot dumplings so it melts around them. Put a spoonful of sour cream or yoghurt on each plate for dipping into.

RABBI MONIQUE MAYER

My favourite Jewish holiday in childhood was Passover: I loved the ceremony, the songs, the story, and the celebration with family. Every year I looked forward to the special foods symbolic of the Passover story: the bitter herb (horseradish) for the bitter slavery that the Hebrews suffered in Egypt; the parsley dipped in salt water for the joy of spring mingled with the sweat and tears of slavery; the shank bone for the Passover offering of old; the matzah (unleavened bread) or 'bread of affliction'; the beitzah (egg) for the priestly festival offering and rebirth; and the sweet paste of apples, walnuts, wine, and honey for the mortar joining the bricks the Hebrews made without straw.

Truth be told, the biggest delight of the evening was not any food tied to the Passover story, but the morsels that came in the starter before the main meal. My mouth would salivate in anticipation of chicken soup with kneidlekh which are Jewish dumplings made from matzah meal, eggs, water, and fat. Kneidlekh come in different textures and consistencies, and everyone has their favourites. One Passover as we celebrated with a room full of families, my mother came out to present the choices. "Okay, who wants the hard balls and who wants the soft balls?" she exclaimed, raising a few eyebrows and smiles. My preference has always been soft, fluffy kneidlekh like my grandmother, then my mother made. My mother revealed that my grandmother added seltzer water to make the kneidlekh expand as they simmered in the pot. But I discovered that simply by following the recipe on the back of a box of matzah meal, mine always came out soft and fluffy.

For as long as I can remember, my family only served kneidlekh at Passover. Every year we'd say "these are so good! Why don't we have these the rest of the year?" and then wouldn't eat them again until the following Passover. I probably started making them during the rest of the year when I went to university. Chicken soup with kneidlekh was nutritious, filling, and easy to make. Over time, this became my comfort food. Eating even one kneidl would bring back the memories of laughter and celebration with family.

Unfortunately, 10 years ago I was forced to move to a wheat-free diet. How could I enjoy chicken soup without my beloved kneidlekh? We tried making them with spelt and then oat flour, but the results were hard and dense and tasted almost entirely unlike kneidlekh. Then my husband, Nigel – the main cook in the family – looked on the internet for alternatives and discovered that kneidlekh could be made with almond flour. The first time he served them was a revelation. Finally, I could have my kneidlekh again. To be honest, it's been so many years since having the real thing that I couldn't tell you if they taste exactly like the kneidlekh from my childhood, but they look like them, they have the same texture, and they are delicious. So here is the basic recipe; we add the cinnamon and nutmeg, which make the kneidlekh even better. You can essentially serve them in any broth. They are very filling, and very moreish!

FOOD AND MEMORIES: THE COMFORT OF KNEIDLEKH
(MY GLUTEN-FREE KNEIDLEKH)

Preparation time: 15 minutes, plus 1 hour resting • Cooking time: 30 minutes • Makes around 20

200g almond flour • 1 tsp salt • ½ tsp pepper • 4 large eggs • ½ tsp ground cinnamon • ½ tsp ground nutmeg

Sift the almond flour into a large bowl, then add the salt and pepper. Add the eggs one at a time, mixing well after each. Lastly, add the cinnamon and nutmeg and whisk up the whole mixture.

Refrigerate the mixture in the bowl for at least 1 hour.

Dip your fingertips in water and form the rested mixture into small balls about 2.5cm (1 inch) in diameter. Drop the kneidlekh into boiling water or broth and let them simmer for about 30 minutes. Serve in soup or broth with 1 to 3 balls per bowl.

ALUEL DE GARANG

My amazing friend Kalpna Woolf has asked me several times to share my recipes from South Sudan, where I grew up before moving to the UK. I didn't want to at first, partly because I was going through a lot of personal stuff which affected my self-confidence and I was worried about people judging me, let alone having to cook for people I didn't know!

But right now, I am bursting with positivity and energy! I know 2020 was a difficult year for all of us, but it gave me time to reflect on what really matters in my life. I feel like I used to as a child growing up, with my parents' support and my siblings' love and the fun we used to have. I love cooking and have done from the age of five or six. I remember hanging around the kitchen begging my late Mama to let me cook with her, bless her. She used to have a small saucepan to heat up milk and she would give me a few of each of the ingredients she was cooking, plonk me on a stool next to her so I could reach the cooker and we'd cook away, me using the milk saucepan.

Mama used to let me help her with baking bread and cakes, chopping vegetables and making homemade peanut butter with our homegrown groundnuts (peanuts) or homemade yoghurt (roope) with fresh milk from our cows. She'd make butter and ghee too, from the separated milk.

The following is one of my favourite South Sudanese recipes. It's served at every event and gathering – be that a wedding, party, funeral or just when friends and family visit – and all my non-South Sudanese friends love it!

So here goes. By the way, I don't follow recipes – neither did my Mama – but I have it all in my head. I am an experimental cook so I hope you can all follow this recipe! I always make it with love, from my heart, with pride and pleasure. Dedicated to my amazing multi-talented late Mama, Anna Athour Kulang, who taught me everything I know about food and cooking.

SUDANESE AUBERGINE SALAD
(SALATA ASWAD, AS IT'S CALLED IN ARABIC)

Preparation time: 20 minutes • Cooking time: 1 hour • Serves 6-8

4 aubergines • 5 tbsp vegetable oil • 2 tins of tomatoes (you can use plum or fresh tomatoes) • 1 Oxo cube • 2 tsp tomato purée • 2 fresh chillies, chopped • Chopped or minced garlic, to taste • 2-3 tbsp peanut butter (I use crunchy, but you can use smooth if you're feeling smooth!) • Salt and pepper • 2 limes or 1 lemon

Preheat the oven to 200°c (Gas Mark 6). Wash the aubergines, then cut them into cubes. Drizzle with the oil, using just enough to coat them, and mix until the aubergines are completely covered. Place them in an ovenproof tray large enough to hold them in one layer, cover with foil so they cook evenly and put them in the oven for about 30 minutes. Some people fry the aubergines, but for me they absorb a lot of oil that way.

While the aubergines are cooking, put the tinned tomatoes into a saucepan (preferably non-stick) on the stove. Add the Oxo cube, tomato purée, chillies, garlic and peanut butter. Bring to the boil, stirring constantly to avoid burning or sticking, then reduce the heat to the lowest setting and let it simmer.

Once the aubergines are cooked through, add them to the saucepan. Mix them into the sauce and leave to simmer for about 10 to 15 minutes. Add salt and pepper to taste.

Halve the limes or lemon and squeeze in the juice, then let it simmer for another 5 minutes and it's done! Eat this with pitta bread, flatbread, crusty French bread (any bread!) or with rice, bulgur wheat, couscous… whatever tickles your fancy!

Bristol has a strong history of twinning with other cities to extend friendships around the world. In 1988, Bristol had the opportunity to twin with Tbilisi, the capital of Georgia, which at the time was part of the Soviet Union but became an independent nation again in 1992. Georgians have a very strong sense of hospitality and a guest is described as 'a gift from God'. I first went to Tbilisi in 1996 as a guest of the Georgian government, and this trip developed into a long-term love of the country, its people and its culture. Georgians will often invite you to a formal meal called a supra, which is a Georgian banquet with fantastic food, wine and music. The most iconic of Georgian dishes is khachapuri, a flatbread filled with cheese for which each region has its own unique recipe. Georgians usually use Imeretian cheese, but this isn't available in the UK so a mixture of mozzarella and cheddar works well instead. Khachapuri reminds me of the best of Georgian cuisine and should be on the must-eat list for anyone who travels to Georgia.

GEORGIAN KHACHAPURI

Preparation time: 40 minutes • Cooking time: 30 minutes • Makes 1

200g bread flour • 1 tbsp sugar • ½ tbsp yeast • ½ tbsp salt • 1 tbsp sunflower oil • 150ml warm water • 110g cheddar cheese, grated • 110g mozzarella cheese, grated • ½ egg, beaten

Combine the flour, sugar, yeast and salt in a large bowl. Pour in the oil and warm water while you mix everything by hand to form a dough. Once it has come together, turn the dough out and knead it for 5 to 8 minutes on a floured board. Alternatively, you can put all the ingredients into a food processor and mix for 2 minutes. Allow the dough to rise in a warm place for 30 minutes.

Mix the two cheeses with the beaten egg in a small bowl. Roll out the dough and place the cheese mixture on top in the centre. Fold over the sides of the dough to form a ball with the cheese in the centre. Roll out lightly again and place the shaped dough on a greased baking tray. Bake in the oven at 170°c for approximately for 25 to 30 minutes until the top is golden brown. Remove the khachapuri from the oven, cut into slices and serve.

ADRIAN KIRIKMAA

There are 91 languages spoken in Bristol and Bristolian is the most spoken language, so it felt fitting to ask one of our celebrated chefs, born and bred in Bristol, to talk about his most cherished memory and recipe.

"I love prawn cocktail as it was one of my first foodie childhood memories. I remember when my aunty took me to St Peter Port in Guernsey in 1978. I was so excited; it was my first time on an aeroplane with propellers and I had never stayed in a hotel before either. We had the breakfast and dinner package, and at the second dinner we were served prawn cocktail. I'd never seen anything like it, growing up in Briz. The only dish I knew was spaghetti bolognese, which I also loved.

Anyway, I was completely blown away by the delicious flavour of the prawn cocktail. I remember discussing how lovely the dish was with my aunty, and I wanted more of it. I've never forgotten that moment and still love prawn cocktail for those reasons. I've changed the recipe since then though; you have to move with the times!"

ADRIAN'S BRIZZLE PRAWN COCKTAIL

This is a relatively simple dish and doesn't take long to prepare. You could also make fresh mayonnaise if preferred.

Preparation time: 20 minutes • Serves 4

100g cucumber • ½ clove of garlic • ¼ fresh chilli • 10g fresh dill • 4 tbsp mayonnaise • 1½ tbsp tomato ketchup • 1 tsp sweet chilli sauce • Pinch of smoked paprika • Pinch of paprika • Pinch of Maldon sea salt • Freshly ground pepper • ½ lemon • 2 little gem lettuces • 300g fresh prawns • Olive oil

First, prepare your ingredients. Peel and finely dice the cucumber and garlic. Finely dice the chilli, removing the seeds if you prefer less heat. Chop the dill and put some aside for garnish. Combine the mayo, ketchup, sweet chilli sauce and both types of paprika with the fresh ingredients. Add sea salt, black pepper and a squeeze of lemon juice to taste.

Wash and dry the lettuces, then break the leaves into bite-size pieces. Ensure the prawns are free of water, lightly squeezing them if necessary. Arrange the lettuce on plate, heap the prawns on top and spoon the cocktail sauce over the prawns. Finish with the reserved dill and a drizzle of olive oil.

KIKI'S ONUGBU SOUP

The recipe I've chosen to share from my Nigerian heritage is onugbu soup (bitter leaf soup). This soup is native to the Igbo tribe where I'm from. Growing up in Nigeria, I often thought that cooking soup was such a big deal because whenever my mum said we needed to make some, the whole day would be spent cooking soup! The process seemed endless because of the time it took to prepare all the necessary ingredients and to cook the different meats and dried fish that made the soup rich in flavour and nutrients.

Preparing to cook onugbu soup was a whole different ball game. Sometimes we started the preparation a day before by washing the bitterness out of the onugbu leaves, which can take some time to do. I have fond memories of picking bitter leaves from our garden and carefully selecting the large healthy-looking ones, then afterwards putting my finger in my mouth only to cringe at the bitter taste the leaves had left. Before we could use the leaves, they had to be mashed and washed several times over, leaving a pile of disintegrated saturated leaves with just a hint of the bitter taste which gives the soup its unique flavour.

Aside from the onugbu leaves and the stock generated by the assortment of cooked meats and dried fish, there is one ingredient that makes onugbu soup a distinctive Igbo soup, and it's called ogiri. Ogiri is made from the paste of fermented oil seeds that adds an aromatic flavour to the soup. When I make onugbu soup here in the UK, I skip adding the ogiri, partly because I don't know where to buy it and partly because I'm not a fan of its pungent scent. The soup still tastes great without it though. Luckily, I can buy bitter leaves that have already been washed and packed, ready to use. So, this soup only takes me only around 1 hour and 10 minutes to make. Here's my version of this Igbo dish.

ONUGBU SOUP

If preferred, you can use the same quantities of beef, lamb or goat meat instead of the chicken and smoked turkey for this dish. Try to match the stock cubes with the meat you're using. Cocoyam are a root vegetable also known as taro, not unlike potatoes in their texture.

Preparation time: 10 minutes • Cooking time: approx. 1 hour • Serves 6-8

---

5 cocoyam • 500g chicken, diced • 3 stock cubes • 500g smoked turkey • 100ml red palm oil • 1½ tbsp ground crayfish • 1 tsp ogiri (optional) • 2 handfuls of bitter leaf, washed and squeezed out • Salt and pepper

Boil the cocoyam until soft. Like potatoes, you know they are done when you stick a fork in and it feels soft. Leave to cool before transferring the cocoyam to a blender, then blend until paste-like.

While the cocoyam cooks, season the chicken with salt and pepper, then place in a large pan. Make up some stock with 2 of the stock cubes according to the instructions on the packet, then pour it over the chicken, ensuring that the liquid is at the same level as the meat. Bring to the boil and cook on a medium heat until the chicken is nearly done, then add the smoked turkey.

Cook the meats in the stock for a further 10 to 15 minutes. When the chicken and turkey are done, remove them from the pan. If you like, brown them in a hot oven for around 20 minutes while the soup cooks, then add the meat back to the pan just before serving.

Reduce the heat under the pan and begin to scoop the cocoyam paste one spoonful at a time into the boiling stock. Simmer on a medium heat, stirring occasionally, while you do this. The cocoyam paste acts as a thickener for the soup.

When the paste has dissolved (which takes around 10 minutes), add the red palm oil, crayfish, remaining stock cube and ogiri (if using). Allow to simmer, stirring as needed. When all the ingredients have been thoroughly mixed and cooked for around 5 minutes, stir in the bitter leaves and cook for a further 5 minutes, then the soup is done.

Serve the onugbu soup with your favourite fufu variety. Fufu is an accompaniment and can be anything, like yams and plantain. I use ground oats as the fufu to my soups, made with finely blended Scottish porridge oats combined with boiling water to the consistency I like, depending on my mood. For a medium-soft fufu, try blending 60g of blended oats with 100ml of boiling water.

SHARING OUR ... FAMILY TIMES

"I would watch as my mom slowly and meticulously sorted through bunches upon bunches of green herbs scattered before her. The aromatic herbs would scent the house as she washed and chopped them. She would then go through the labour-intensive steps of making the perfect fluffy rice, nailing it each time and making a mountain of rice with the perfect amount of herbs and butter to coat each grain."
– Anita Ayrom

TRADITIONAL ERITREAN BUN CEREMONY

My family and I migrated to Sweden from Eritrea when I was a young girl. Sweden became our new home, where we settled down and built our new life. We grew up always having people around us, especially Eritrean people, though when we first arrived there wasn't a very large Eritrean community like there is nowadays. We had an open-door policy where we cooked and shared what we had with others. My mum always cooked and invited me and my siblings to help in the kitchen. Everyone had a role but being the youngest of six, I had the smallest role. I learned quickly and knew that I wanted a bigger responsibility in the kitchen, from stirring the big pot to using the knife. My mum was a talented cook. She always made a big pot of food and shared it with neighbours and extended family. We also always had food in the freezer in case anyone was hungry. Food and socialising are at the centre of our culture.

Zigni with injera is the main traditional dish of Eritrean cuisine. Eritrea and Ethiopia have many similar cuisines because of people's history. Zigni is a beef stew in a tomato sauce flavoured with berbere, a rather hot spice blend full of flavour that accompanies almost every dish. Injera is a round loaf of bread, with a spongy consistency and a slightly sour taste due to its slow fermentation. It's made with teff flour or millet flour and is used in place of cutlery to scoop the stew into your mouth.

I cooked it for the first time by myself when I left home to study in Bristol. There were no Eritrean restaurants and so I had to cook zigni for me and my friends. I called my mum often to make

sure I was doing it right, especially the injera as it needs to ferment. Most of my friends had never tasted anything like it and I know that even if it didn't go exactly right, at least it tasted good. When I used to go back to Sweden for my holidays, my mum would freeze different Eritrean dishes and give them to me to take to England and eat with my friends.

In Eritrea and Ethiopia, we also have a traditional coffee ceremony called bun. The coffee is offered when visiting friends during festivals, or as a part of daily life. Fresh coffee beans are roasted until dark and then offered around the room for guests and family to smell. The coffee is then ground, and ginger is added before the coffee is placed in the jebena, a clay pot used for pouring the prepared coffee. It is served in small cups called finjal, accompanied by sugar. The coffee grounds are brewed three times: the first round of coffee is called awel in Tigrinya (meaning first), the second kalaay (meaning second) and the third bereka (meaning 'to be blessed'). Additionally, etan (a fragrant, incense-like ingredient also known as powdered gum Arabic) is burned atop hot charcoal to create a wonderful aroma in the room.

We used to drink it at the weekend, my family and I in Sweden. I would wake to the smell of the bun and realise that it was time for long hours around the sofa, drinking and catching up with the whole family. The first cup is always given to the oldest in the room as a sign of respect.

ERITREAN ZIGNI WITH HOMEMADE BERBERE SPICE BLEND

Here is my recipe for Zigni and the spices I use to make my berbere blend.

Preparation time: 20-30 minutes • Cooking time: 1 hour 30 minutes • Serves 4-6

For the berbere • 1 cup (approx. 142g) red chilli powder • 1 tbsp cayenne • 1 tsp onion powder • 1 tsp each ground ginger, cumin, coriander, cardamom and fenugreek • ½ tsp garlic powder • ½ tsp each ground cinnamon, allspice and cloves • ¼ tsp ground nutmeg

For the zigni • 1kg beef • 3 onions • 4 plum tomatoes • 4 cloves of garlic • Knob of fresh ginger • 6 tbsp olive oil • 2 tbsp tomato purée • ½ cup (125ml) water • Pinch of salt • Ground black pepper

For the berbere

Simply mix all the ingredients together and store the spice blend in an airtight jar in the fridge. This will keep for 6 months.

For the zigni

First, cut the beef into bite-size cubes, then dice the onions and plum tomatoes (keeping them separate). Peel and then grate or finely chop the garlic and ginger.

Heat up the oil in a deep pan, then fry the diced onion until dark golden brown. Add 2 tablespoons of the berbere spice blend, mix well and cook on a low heat for 1 or 2 minutes.

Add the cubed beef, diced tomatoes and tomato purée to the pan. Cook for a few minutes before stirring in the garlic and ginger. Continue cooking on a medium to low heat, stirring often. If anything sticks to the bottom of the pan, add a tablespoon or two of water.

After 30 minutes, add the water and season the stew with salt and pepper to taste. Bring to the boil and then cook on a low heat for another 45 minutes, until the beef is tender and soft.

When it's ready, leave the zigni to rest for 10 minutes before serving with injera or other bread.

SOMALI LAMB HUURIS

(RICE WITH MEAT, VEGETABLES, TAMARIND AND YOGHURT)

Preparation time: 25 minutes • Cooking time: 1 hour 30 minutes, depending on the cut of lamb • Serves 5

150ml oil • 3 onions • 3 cardamon pods, lightly opened • 1 stick of cinnamon • 4 cloves of garlic • ½ tsp allspice • ½ tsp ground cumin • ½ tsp grated fresh ginger • 1 tsp salt • Sprinkle of black pepper • 2 vegetarian stock cubes • 2 tbsp tamarind paste • 1kg lamb, cubed • 300g basmati rice • 2 tbsp yoghurt • 3 large potatoes, cubed • 4 carrots, sliced • Handful of fresh coriander • Handful of raisins, to garnish

I met Kalpna at a Refugee Women of Bristol event where she was asking the women if they wanted to take part in the upcoming Peace Feast. Refugee Women of Bristol is a safe space for refugee women to meet and get support. They are also given a free lunch which is cooked by volunteers, and the Peace Feast is Bristol's First International Peace Café feast. I asked her if we could have a dish from each country at the event, and from there I became a volunteer and started cooking Somali food at the charity's supper club.

The food I cook for the supper clubs includes Somali dishes like lamb huuris, served with samosa and salad for starters. Huuris is a popular rice dish in northern Somalia. It's usually served on special occasions, but when I moved to Europe it became a regular within my household. I was taught to make it by my mother, who grew up with her aunties and was taught to cook and tailor by them because she couldn't attend school. My mum used to sew curtains and dresses for people and when there was a big celebration that needed catering for, she was the right person to ask because she was known for making delicious food too. After my mum married, she used these skills to help out and make extra earnings for her family.

When I was six years old, she taught me how to sew clothes and how to cook, the same way her aunties did for her. When I got married and moved to Denmark, I worked in the kitchen of a Danish restaurant where I taught them to make huuris and various other Somali dishes. Surprisingly, people really enjoyed the food and it was regularly in demand. As a mother of five, I have since taught my own children to cook, including my daughter who now has a family of her own.

Heat the oil in a large pan while you finely chop the onions. Fry them on a medium heat with the cardamom and cinnamon until the onion turns brown. Peel and chop the garlic, then add to the pan with the spices, grated ginger, salt, pepper and stock cubes. Mix well and turn the heat down low, then cover the pan and leave it to cook gently for 10 minutes.

Stir in the tamarind paste, then season the cubed lamb with salt before adding it to the pan. Leave to cook until almost tender, then taste to check the seasoning.

While the lamb cooks, wash the rice until the water runs clear, then leave it to soak in salted water for 5 minutes. Drain the rice and par-cook in boiling water.

While the rice cooks, stir the yoghurt into the lamb mixture. Drain the half-cooked rice in a sieve, then add it to the pan and mix gently. Cover the pan with a lid or kitchen foil and leave it on a very low heat for 20 minutes. Meanwhile, fry the potatoes and carrots separately until tender.

After this time, check whether the rice is cooked. Be aware that if the rice is cooked for too long, the sauce will evaporate. Place a large serving plate over the pan and flip over so the rice is below the sauce. Garnish with the coriander and raisins, then serve alongside the potatoes and carrots.

ANITA'S SABZI POLO BA MAHI

Few things can elicit the deeply intense memories that certain foods can evoke. My mother's sabzi polo ba mahi (herbed rice with fish) serves as a backdrop for a wealth of childhood memories.

This is the staple dish for the Iranian Nowruz (New Year) and is served as lunch or dinner on the first day of spring. The philosophy of this dish is attributed to the symbolism of the ingredients: fish for liveliness, fresh herbs for spring and rice as a representation of our blessings.

I would watch as my mom slowly and meticulously sorted through bunches upon bunches of green herbs scattered before her. The aromatic herbs would scent the house as she washed and chopped them. She would then go through the labour-intensive steps of making the perfect fluffy rice, nailing it each time and making a mountain of rice with the perfect amount of herbs and butter to coat each grain. Then came the fish, which almost seemed secondary to the rice in my household.

Having moved to Canada when I was 5 years old, my connection to Iran is and has been ambiguous, to say the least. My parents' accents, school lunches, and the scents coming from my mother's kitchen were constant reminders that we were different, that I was different. This divide grew further with my parents' opposing beliefs. While my mother was more traditional, my father leaned towards atheism. However, Nowruz was the one holiday that my whole family was quick to embrace. The disconnect in religion, race and language did not impede the celebration, because Nowruz was not about any of those things. It was about nature and new beginnings; and that was something we all valued.

After my father's passing, I grew to appreciate this dish more and more; it takes me back to when we were all around the table, counting our blessings and enjoying a lovely, fragrant, delicious meal together.

SABZI POLO BA MAHI
(PERSIAN AROMATIC HERBED RICE WITH FISH)

This is mine and my mom's favourite recipe, I hope you enjoy cooking it as much as I do.

Preparation time: 3 hours • Cooking time: I hour 30 minutes • Serves 4-5

For the sabzi polo • 400g long grain basmati rice • 6 tbsp salt • ½ bunch of dill • ½ bunch of parsley • ½ bunch of coriander • ½ bunch of spring onions • ⅓ bunch of spinach • 4-5 cloves of garlic • ½ tsp ground saffron • 3 tbsp vegetable oil • 3 tbsp butter or ghee

For the mahi • I white fleshed fish (such as seabass, trout or branzino) • ½ tsp each salt, pepper and paprika • ¼ tsp each ground turmeric and garlic powder • I lemon, thinly sliced

For the sabzi polo

Cover the rice with water and stir gently with your fingers. Drain, rinse and repeat between 2 and 5 times until the water runs clear. Soak the washed rice in 2 litres of lukewarm water with 4 tablespoons of the salt for at least I hour. The longer it soaks, the fluffier the grains will be. Meanwhile, thoroughly wash and then finely chop all the fresh herbs, spring onions and spinach. Peel and finely chop the garlic, then combine it with the herb mixture.

Dissolve the ground saffron in 4 tablespoons of hot water and set aside. In a large non-stick pot, bring 1.2 litres of water with the remaining 2 tablespoons of salt to the boil. Drain the soaked rice, tip into the pot and stir briefly. After about 3 minutes, add the garlic and herb mixture to the pot and stir thoroughly. Continue to cook until the rice is tender outside but still firm to the bite, about 3 to 4 more minutes. Drain the rice in a colander, rinse with cool water and set aside.

Wash and dry the pot, then add the vegetable oil and 2 tablespoons of the saffron water and place on a medium heat. Gently place the herbed rice back into the pot in a pyramid shape, ensuring the base of the pot is completely covered. Gently make 4 holes in the rice with the handle of a wooden spoon to allow the steam to escape while cooking. Pour 115ml of water around the edges, then cover and cook for about 10 minutes or until you see steam escaping. Add 3 tablespoons of butter or ghee and the remaining saffron water to the rice. Reduce the heat to medium-low, cover and cook for about 50 to 60 minutes.

For the mahi

Clean, gut and scale the fish. Make a few cuts on both sides, then gently rub the salt, pepper, paprika, turmeric and garlic powder over the whole fish. Lay 2 or 3 lemon slices on top, cover and leave it to marinate for at least I hour. About 30 minutes before the rice is ready, preheat the oven to 450°c. Place the marinated fish on an oiled tray and bake for about 20 to 25 minutes or until crispy and golden. Optionally, grill the fish for the last 2 to 4 minutes for extra crispiness.

To serve

Serve the rice on a platter. Flip the pot upside down to reveal the tahdig (crispy rice) and place on a separate plate. Place the fish on the side of the plate or in a separate dish. Serve with pickled garlic or vegetables and radishes and fresh herbs on the side.

MOH'S LOVE, ROMANCE AND DRIED LIMES GHORMEH SABZI

Preparation time: 30 minutes
• Cooking time: 2 hours 20 minutes • Serves 4

5 tbsp sunflower oil • 3 onions, finely chopped • 900g (2lb) lamb shoulder, cubed and fat trimmed off • I tsp ground turmeric • Salt and pepper • 50g each fresh fenugreek, coriander, chives, parsley and spinach, chopped • 6 dried limes, each pricked a few times • I tin of kidney beans

Heat 3 tablespoons of the oil in a saucepan and fry the chopped onion gently until soft. Add the cubed lamb and let it brown on all sides before stirring in the turmeric, salt and pepper.

In a separate pan, heat the remaining oil. When hot, fry the chopped herbs and spinach on a medium heat for 3 to 4 minutes, stirring continuously.

Pour cold water into the first pan so the lamb is completely covered, and then add the fried herb mixture. Bring to the boil, then reduce to a simmer and cook for I hour.

After this time, add the dried limes. Cook for another hour (adding a little water if the stew looks too dry) until the sauce has thickened and the meat is tender.

A few minutes before serving, drain the kidney beans, stir them into the stew and cook until heated through. Serve the gormeh sabzi with saffron rice.

Ghormeh sabzi is more than Iran's signature dish, it's part of the country's national identity. This dish combines cubed lamb cooked slowly with an abundance of chopped fresh herbs – parsley, chives, coriander, fenugreek – with soft kidney beans and a special Iranian ingredient – dried limes, adding a sour and tangy flavour – which brought two people from different parts of the world together. Moh remembers: "When I first came to this country, I really missed my home food. So, I started to cook some of the dishes we used to eat as a family. My friends would come around and enjoy the food so much that they encouraged me to start to sell some of the food. One day, a Dutch woman called Christien came and said that she had tried my ghormeh sabzi and had been intrigued by new flavours she had never tasted before (it was the dried limes!). Christien became a regular customer, and we would eat together and talk about food. Over time, we met more often and love blossomed between us. I wanted to share our love of Persian food with people in this country and so we opened a Persian café together and I am still cooking dishes from my heritage, and of course, my wife Christien's favourite ghormeh sabzi headlines the menu.

Family meals are so important in our home: a time to sit down and share good conversation, any worries and happiness, always around a big wooden table with a collection of wonky chairs in various stages of repair. A steaming plate of delicious food would come together in the chaos of the day and a moment would always be had before diving in, to give thanks for the food we had and think of those who did not.

Cooking was part of growing up, happily helping Mum chop an array of veggies or mixing up cake batter to bake in the ancient Aga on the farm. All the food was gathered from tiny local shops, the vegetable patch and often directly from the river by my dad or brother. Spices and herbs were often added to the more traditional meals of meat, potatoes and two veggies, influenced by my mother's childhood with her parents. She spent a lot of time in Zimbabwe (then Rhodesia) and Jerusalem, as did I, where colours, spices, smells and tastes brought the senses alive.

The 'one tray bake' is quick and easy for busy big families, as well as being cost effective and super tasty. I still love cooking this for friends and sharing it with clients. You can't really go wrong by changing the veggies and proteins to your taste and mixing it up with a simple tomato or chilli sauce if you wish. This is great energised food for all.

FROM JERUSALEM TO SCOTLAND
KIM'S ENERGISED ONE TRAY BAKE

You can swap the salmon for chicken or just use veggies here. I always cook more than needed as it lasts for several meals, plus the larger pieces of fish are less tampered with and work out cheaper overall. Go for organic and local produce, ethically sourced if you can.

Preparation time: 15 minutes
• Cooking time: approx. 30-45 minutes • Serves 4

I tub of samphire (optional) • 2 leeks, finely chopped • Small handful of kale • ¼ red cabbage, sliced • 4 large ethically sourced salmon fillets • I courgette, diced • 3 cloves of garlic, crushed • 2 tbsp grated fresh ginger • I large red onion, finely chopped • I red chilli, finely chopped (optional) • I tin of chickpeas or I medium sweet potato, finely chopped • I large handful of chestnut or white mushrooms • 2 tsp ground turmeric • I tsp dried oregano • 2 tbsp coconut oil or a drizzle of olive oil • I lemon or lime, halved

Spread the samphire, leeks, kale and cabbage out on a large baking tray and lay the salmon fillets on top. Scatter the diced courgette, crushed garlic, grated ginger, chopped onion and chilli (if using) around the salmon. Drain and rinse the chickpeas then add them to the tray or distribute the sweet potato over the other vegetables, along with the mushrooms.

Season everything with the turmeric and oregano, then drizzle over the coconut oil (it may be easier to melt this first) or olive oil. Squeeze over the lemon or lime juice so everything is evenly covered.

Cover the whole tray with tin foil and place in a preheated oven at 180°c to bake for 20 minutes. After this time, remove the foil and bake uncovered for another 10 minutes. Timings will vary depending on the size of the fish or meat fillets and how well-done you like them, so adapt and keep checking as needed.

Serve warm with cooked wild rice or steamed spinach on the side. Alternatively, it can be left to cool and refrigerated, then eaten as a salad for lunch the next day.

MARIA'S CYPRIOT ANTINAXTO KRASATO

My mother, Maria, was born on 29th October 1937 in a village called Trikomo, in Cyprus, which unfortunately has been illegally occupied since 1974 when the Turkish government invaded Cyprus (a story for another time!). By the age of nine Maria had lost her father and was kept at home by her mother to look after her two younger sisters, meaning she did not go to school. Her education as a mother started early, as it was her job to look after her sisters while her mother went out to work.

At the age of 16 Maria was sent to Bristol, in England, to work with other Cypriots as her mother could not afford to feed them all. This was where her cooking experiences really started, as the work was in the restaurant and café business. By today's standards, you would almost call it modern day slavery, but she had a roof over her head, food to eat and clothes to wear, and for that she was thankful. Maria met her husband, Pavlos, in England. He was also from Cyprus and had also left to find greater opportunities.

Soon after meeting, they opened their first restaurant, the Horsefair Restaurant and Greek Taverna on the Horsefair parade in the city centre. They then moved onto the Bellapais Taverna on Alma Vale Road in Clifton. Of course, they specialised in Cypriot cuisine.

The kitchen became known as Maria's kitchen. Customers would not be happy until they walked into "Maria's Kitchen" and checked with the boss what the dish of the day was, much to my dad's disappointment! In many cases, my mother would prepare off-menu traditional meals when produce allowed. The one dish that not only our customers but the whole family loved was her antinaxto, with pork and potatoes. To this day her grandchildren and great grandchildren love this dish and long for those juicy and succulent potatoes and lean pork chops... delicious! I always remember, even after having my own family, looking forward to and rushing to see Mum and Dad just to eat antinaxto with them! We all love this dish.

Sadly, Maria has been struck with Alzheimer's and is not able to cook for us anymore. What's amazing is that all the family – three siblings, eight grandkids and all the great grandkids – try to replicate this dish. Only two weeks ago my son Pavlos was asking me what to do and when and how to crack the potatoes. My brother George also commented on the recipe and how it's wonderful that Mum's cooking always brings us together with great memories.

MARIA'S CYPRIOT ANTINAXTO KRASATO (TOSSED PORK OR CHICKEN WITH POTATOES)

An extremely traditional Cypriot 'village style' main dish. Written by an artisan, not a professional…

Preparation time: 30 minutes, plus marinating overnight • Cooking time: 1 hour 30 minutes • Serves 4

---

8 boneless chicken thighs, halved or 700g pork, cubed (pork shoulder is good) • ¼ bottle of red wine • 10 tbsp cooking oil • 1kg new potatoes, washed and scrubbed but not peeled • 4 tbsp crushed coriander seeds • Salt and pepper, to taste • 500g whole button mushrooms • 2-3 lemons, to serve (optional)

The night before you want to cook this dish, marinate your chosen meat in the red wine. The next day, put the oil into a large pot or pan. Gently crack, not crush, your potatoes into the pan. Do not smother the potatoes in oil, just let them sit in it. This will allow them to soak up the flavour. Fry them in the pot until golden brown, being careful not to break or crush them. When golden brown, take them out and place on a plate, ready to go back into the pot once the meat is ready.

Next, add some of the red wine marinade to the cooking oil in the pot, along with the meat. Brown the meat, but don't cook it all the way through. Add the coriander and seasoning to taste. Once the meat is ready, add the potatoes and rest of the marinade to the pot, plus more red wine if you wish!

Once both the potatoes and meat have been thoroughly browned, the dish will need around 35 to 45 minutes to cook through. You should ensure there is sufficient marinade or wine to cover the solids, so the liquid should be half to three quarters of the contents. You must not stir this dish but toss the contents as you cook. This is where the name antinaxto (meaning tossed) comes from. Therefore, it is best to have a lid although this is not necessary for the experienced Cypriot cook!

When the dish is almost finished cooking, add the whole button mushrooms, again tossing the contents together. Ensure the heat is fairly low towards the end so that you don't overcook anything. Your potatoes should not break up; if they start to do so then your dish is more than ready.

Finally, decant the dish into a serving bowl by pouring it in quickly to avoid the potatoes breaking up. Don't spoon it out of the pot, as the potatoes will be incredibly soft and succulent. When eating this delicious dish you may want to add a squeeze of lemon, or Cyprus juice as we call it! Kali orexi (enjoy)!

It was always exciting when we were getting kadhi at home. It was a firm family favourite. I remember in summertime when we all got together, it used to be everyone's first choice for dinner. Back then, kadhi used to be made with buttermilk. I remember my mother churning the milk, taking the butter out of it and saving some of the buttermilk for us to drink. On some days my mother would announce she was going to make kadhi and we would look forward to eating it on top of a mound of rice.

The heart of the kadhi is the pakoras, a kind of delicious, spicy vegetable fritter. In the monsoon season, pakoras are made in every household as a hot snack. It's hard to resist pakoras when you are making kadhi; they can get eaten before the khadi is ready, so make extra pakoras when you are preparing this!

Even now in my house we love this dish and I love to make it for my wife, Saroj, my children Sachin and Sarika and my grandson, Devin. My mouth is watering already writing about it. I think today is definitely going to be a kadhi day!

The hallmark of a good kadhi is that it should have a sour, tangy and spicy taste. To give it the tangy flavour, we leave natural yoghurt outside the fridge for 1 or 2 days and add a sprinkle of salt. If you can't do this, try to buy tangy natural yoghurt.

PUNJABI KADHI WITH PAKORAS

Preparation time: 15-20 minutes • Cooking time: 30 minutes • Serves 4

For the pakoras • 4-5 cauliflower florets • 1 medium onion • 1 medium carrot • 1 large potato • 50g spinach leaves • ½ tbsp ground turmeric • 1 tsp ground coriander • 1 tsp ajwain (carom) seeds • 1 tsp chaat masala • ½ tsp garam masala • Pinch of red chilli powder • ½ tsp salt • 100g gram flour • 1 litre vegetable oil

For the kadhi • 1kg full-fat natural yoghurt • 150g gram flour • 1 tsp ground turmeric • ½ tsp red chilli powder • 8-10 tbsp vegetable oil • 1 large onion • 2.5cm (1 inch) fresh ginger • 3 cloves of garlic • 1 tbsp coriander seeds • 2 black cardamom pods • 1½ tsp fenugreek seeds • 1 tsp cumin seeds • 1 tsp garam masala • 1 tsp salt

For the pakoras

First, thinly slice the cauliflower florets and finely chop the onion. Dice the carrot and potato, then wash and roughly chop the spinach. Place all the prepared vegetables in a bowl, then sprinkle over the spices and salt. Mix thoroughly and then add the gram flour, a tablespoon of the oil and enough water to bring the mixture together. Make sure the batter completely coats the vegetables.

Heat the remaining oil in a deep pan. Carefully drop a tablespoon of the pakora mixture into the hot oil. Repeat but don't overcrowd the pan. You should be able to make about 20 pakoras. Fry them in batches until golden brown and then drain on paper towels.

For the kadhi

Put the yoghurt in a large bowl and whisk by hand until smooth. Add the gram flour and continue whisking thoroughly until the mixture has a smooth batter consistency. Whisk in the turmeric and chilli powder, making sure there are no lumps.

Heat the oil in a large saucepan while you slice the onion, peel and grate the ginger, then crush the garlic cloves and coriander seeds. Fry the onion in the hot oil until soft, then add the ginger, garlic, coriander, cardamom pods, remaining spices and salt.

When the onions have browned, pour in the gram flour and yoghurt mixture. Bring to a gentle boil and then reduce to a simmer for 15 minutes until it thickens. Now add the pakoras to the pan and turn the heat off. Let the kadhi sit for 5 minutes before serving with plain rice.

NONNA BIANCHI'S IRISH LAMB STEW

As a young boy, I was in love with food from the very beginning. I'm from a family of five siblings and have lots of cousins, so dinner time was noisy at the Mill where I grew up, and still live with my wife and twin daughters. The story, as my mum would tell it, is that during those raucous meals my eyes never left the plate, even with a mob of children running riot around me.

Although born in Bristol, my heritage is diverse with roots in Scotland, Ireland, Italy and India. I think that all these cultures impacted the way my parents brought me up, but perhaps the Italian and Indian influence made sure food and family were forever woven together for me, as indeed they are for my own children, Annie-May and Betsy.

My Italian Nonno sadly passed away before any of his grandchildren were born. He was a highly trained chef and restaurant manager from Lago di Como, in the Northern Lake district of Italy. My mum has many colourful stories of what life was like growing up in a council estate in Bristol in the 60s, with an Italian father and Scots/Irish mother who had met while working in the same hotel.

Although money was very often tight, meals at home never reflected this it seems. Nonno would make fresh pasta and hang strips of tagliatelle over the backs of chairs, and chunky white bread was always on the table with pools of olive oil in little bowls waiting for it to be dipped into. Mum and her sisters drank water and wine. The girls' friends would be amazed by how different mealtimes were in their house compared to their own. Undoubtedly, the experiences of my mum and aunties translated into the big family gatherings with food for all to share that characterised my youth.

Although none of the four sisters had lasting careers in the hospitality sector, all of them worked in bars and restaurants as they grew up. Nonna worked in the Llandoger Trow back in the Bristol hey-day of Berni Inns: duck in orange sauce and battered scampi. And now, in 2021, the third generation of Bianchis own and run five restaurants here in Bristol: Pasta Loco, Pasta Ripiena, La Sorella, Bianchis and Adelina Yard. Our ancestry is a reason to be grateful for so much.

Although my Nonno was the qualified chef, Nonna was also a highly accomplished home cook hence the recipes I have shared in this book. It is, in fact, my Nonna who I have to thank for being the greatest influence on my career choice, my work ethic and the passion which I have for the food industry across all its domains.

NONNA BIANCHI'S IRISH LAMB STEW

My first recipe is for a dish that our Nonna (she may not be Italian but the name for grandmother stuck) used to cook for us weekly at home. The smell of this stew cooking on my return home from school will forever stay with me.

Preparation time: 30 minutes • Cooking time: 2 hours • Serves 4

1kg diced stewing lamb (lamb neck works well) • Salt and pepper • Small knob of butter • 250g smoked streaky bacon or pancetta lardons • 5 medium white onions, sliced • 5 carrots, cut into chunks • 5 sticks of celery, sliced • 1 swede, cut into 2.5cm (1 inch) dice • 3 bay leaves • 2 sprigs of rosemary • Small bunch of thyme • Splash of white wine • 850ml lamb stock • 6 Maris Piper potatoes, peeled and quartered • 5 sprigs of parsley, chopped

Preheat the oven to 180°c. Season the lamb generously with salt and pepper, then in a heavy-based casserole pan on a high heat, cook the lamb in the butter for 5 minutes. Caramelise the meat on all sides, then remove it from the pan and set aside.

Add the bacon to the same pan and cook for 3 minutes to render some of the fat and brown the meat, before setting it aside with lamb. Next, add the prepared vegetables and herbs to the pan along with a splash of white wine, stirring occasionally to ensure they do not catch.

Cook the vegetables for 5 minutes before adding the meat back to the pan along with the lamb stock. Bring to the boil then drop the heat to a simmer. Place the potatoes on top of the stew then cover the pan with a lid. Transfer the casserole to the preheated oven and cook for 2 hours, or until the meat is tender to the touch.

When the stew is ready, stir in the chopped parsley, season to taste with salt and pepper, then serve with a big slice of buttered brown bread.

OUR FAMILY'S CHICKEN MILANESE WITH SPAGHETTI

My second recipe is breaded chicken with spaghetti in garlic, chilli, parsley and olive oil. A classic dish from Italy, and my absolute personal favourite: timeless comfort food at its best. Before my daughters Annie-May and Betsy made the honourable decision to become vegetarian, it was a big favourite of theirs too.

Preparation time: 15 minutes • Cooking time: 30 minutes • Serves 4

---

2 skinless chicken breasts, halved lengthways • 2 eggs • Splash of milk • 100g plain flour, seasoned generously with salt and pepper • 250g breadcrumbs • Olive oil, for shallow frying • 400g dry spaghetti • 5 cloves of garlic, finely chopped • 2 red chillies, deseeded and finely chopped • ½ bunch of flat leaf parsley, roughly chopped • Parmesan, finely grated • 2 lemons, halved

Begin by flattening each piece of chicken to tenderise it, preferably with a meat hammer or a hard utensil such as a rolling pin. This is best done between two sheets of cling film to protect the meat so it doesn't tear on impact.

Put the eggs and milk into a mixing bowl and whisk well. Next, dip the flattened chicken into the seasoned flour, ensuring it is well coated, then into the egg mix and lastly into the breadcrumbs. Repeat this process with all 4 pieces of chicken.

To cook the chicken, add a good glug of olive oil to a frying pan on a medium heat. Just as the oil starts to really heat up, carefully add the coated chicken to the pan, ensuring it isn't overcrowded (cook in batches if necessary). Cook for 4 minutes on either side until golden.

Meanwhile, boil a generously salted pot of water and cook the pasta according to the instructions on the packaging, reserving the strained cooking water at the end.

While the pasta and chicken are cooking, shallow fry the garlic and chilli with a good splash of olive oil in a saucepan until the garlic turns golden, at which point add the cooked spaghetti to the pan. Using tongs, coat the pasta in the garlicy oil and then add the fresh parsley, a handful of finely grated parmesan and a ladleful of the reserved cooking water. Continue turning the spaghetti in this sauce for 1 minute to give it a glossy finish.

Season the pasta to taste and serve the breaded chicken alongside the spaghetti, offering up half a lemon each to squeeze over the whole dish. Extra parmesan and bread to mop up the plates is always a must in my house and restaurants alike!

TARA'S KURDISH BAMYA
(LAMB AND OKRA STEW)

When buying fresh okra, small or medium pods are the best option. You can also use frozen okra in this recipe.

Preparation time: 30 minutes
• Cooking time: 1 hour 30 minutes • Serves 4

1kg mixed lamb, cubed • 6 tbsp oil • 4 cloves of garlic, finely chopped • 3 dried limes • 2 tins of chopped tomatoes • 400g fresh okra, stems trimmed • Salt and pepper • 2 lemons, juiced

In a heavy pot with a lid, sauté the cubed lamb in 3 to 4 tablespoons of the oil until browned, then cover in hot water and bring to the boil. Skim off the foam that is produced, put the lid on the pot and let it gently simmer on a low heat for 1 hour until the meat is tender.

Transfer the cooked lamb and broth into separate bowls, then heat the remaining oil in the pot. Add the finely chopped garlic and dried limes, stir for 30 seconds and then put the lamb back into the pot. If you would prefer a smoother stew at the end, blend the chopped tomatoes before adding them to the pot, along with 1 cup of the lamb broth. Simmer for 15 minutes on a medium-low heat.

Add the okra to the stew, season with salt and pepper to your liking and then continue to simmer for 20 to 30 minutes. After this time, pour in the lemon juice and simmer for another 5 minutes. Your bamya is ready when the sauce is rich and has thickened up a little. Taste a piece of okra and if it's tender and cooked through, your stew is ready to enjoy!

Serve with plain white rice and salad. Bamya can also be served as a tashreeb, by putting bite-size pieces of flatbread (such as naan) into a bowl, drenching them with bamya sauce and then arranging the meat and slices of onion on top.

Bamya reminds me of my childhood and of warmth and comfort in cold winter days, returning home from school, college or university to smell and find bamya simmering away for us to enjoy. Bamya reminds me of family and communal sharing of food, which is the norm in my Kurdish culture. Bamya reminds me of Kurdistan. It's almost a symbol of the rich, nourishing and wholesome energy I feel when I am among Kurdish people or in Kurdistan.

Time has passed and now my own children hover around in the kitchen and can't wait for bamya to finish cooking so they can devour it! It's the sort of dish that will fill your whole home with its mouth-watering scent and I promise that everyone in your household will ask you "is it ready yet?" until it is. This flavour-filled recipe tastes even better the next day and will convert any doubters of okra!

Photo: @JonCraig_Photos

FROM KALPNA TO CHRISTINA
MY MUM'S CHANA AND SPINACH DAL

This dal can be eaten either as a one-bowl dinner or as a soup. It tastes even better the next day so make double the quantity. Serve with rice or chapati.

Preparation time: 15 minutes, plus minimum 1 hour soaking • Cooking time: 1 hour • Serves 4

200g (7oz) chana dal • 2 litres water • 2 tsp ground turmeric

For the sauce • 8 tbsp olive oil • 30g (1oz) butter (optional) • 1 tbsp cumin seeds • 4 cloves of garlic, finely chopped • 5cm (2 inches) fresh ginger, peeled and grated • 1 medium onion, finely chopped • 28g fresh coriander, stems and leaves chopped separately • 1 green chilli, finely chopped • 1 tsp ground coriander • ½ tsp chilli powder • ¾ tsp salt • 200g tinned chopped tomatoes, blended • 2 tbsp tomato purée • 4-5 tbsp warm water • 160g spinach leaves, roughly chopped

Dal means nourishment. It signifies life and is a crucial staple in Hindu households. This is my mum's recipe for chana dal, a 'meaty' dal with a wonderful texture which we would look forward to eating as a family. During the week, when my father and mother both worked, my mum would choose the quick-cooking dals for our meals. As chana dal takes a little longer, and is considered an expensive dal, this was a weekend treat or a dal saved for when guests came. It often has spinach or courgettes added to it. My mum would say: "this is not any dal – this is the queen of dals! Take time and love and it will feed you with love."

So, it seemed fitting that I dedicate this recipe to one of our 91 Ways ambassadors, Christina Robino, who sadly passed away last year. It's hard to sum up Christina in a few words; she was a firecracker, a huge force, a connector, relentlessly energetic, kind, an activist for good and an icon in our city. A few years ago, I made this at a dal festival in Bristol and Christina loved it. Later when her mother passed away, she asked me to cook this for the family and friends after the funeral, so I would like to dedicate this to her – a cherished recipe – to say thank you to Christina for nourishing and supporting 91 Ways.

Rinse the dal so the water runs clear, then soak in a bowl of cold water for at least 1 hour, or overnight. Drain the soaked dal and bring the 2 litres of fresh water to the boil in a large saucepan. When the water starts to boil, add the dal and half a teaspoon of the ground turmeric. Partially cover the pan and cook over a medium-high heat for 30 minutes. The water may need skimming if any scum forms on the surface. After 30 minutes, turn up the heat to high and cook for a further 10 to 15 minutes until the dal is soft and the water has been absorbed. The dal should retain its shape but still be soft. If it gets dry, add more hot water.

Meanwhile, heat the oil (and butter if using) in a deep frying pan over a medium heat. Add the cumin seeds and then, as soon as they start to sizzle, add the garlic and ginger. Stir for 1 minute then add the chopped onion, coriander stems and green chilli. Cook for 4 to 5 minutes until the onion is soft and almost brown. Add the remaining turmeric, ground coriander, chilli powder and salt. Stir for 1 or 2 minutes before adding the blended tinned tomatoes, tomato purée and warm water. Leave everything to meld together for about 10 minutes over a low-medium heat until the sauce is thick. At this stage, add the spinach leaves and cook for 1 to 2 minutes until wilted.

When the dal is soft, spoon the sauce into the dal and simmer on a very low heat for 15 minutes. The dal will thicken. Fold in the coriander leaves and serve.

My mother was a fine artist. She produced her work through a variety of mediums throughout her lifetime but one that was steadfast was through her cooking; she was a fantastic cook, meticulous and insightful in her creations. She could literally make a mountain out of a molehill, a talent I am proud to have inherited. I love using creativity to guide me when cooking and find it doesn't fail to yield the best results.

Artist parents can be drawn heavily to their work, meaning that their focus isn't always on the children. The times that I felt my mother's love and presence stronger than any other was when she cooked for me. Her love nourished me through the food she made, which was always revered, and left a blanket of comfort in its wake. It's a pleasure to share one of these filling recipes from my mother, who has been gone three years this month but is not forgotten. I still make this for my family today.

BARBARA JOHNSON'S NUTMEG CHICKEN & RICE BAKE

Preparation time: 25 minutes • Cooking time: 45 minutes • Serves 4

240g white rice • 20g butter • 220g flour • 3g salt • 1g black pepper • 5-7 chicken thighs • 125ml oil • 3 eggs • 375ml milk • 2g nutmeg

Preheat the oven to 180°c. Meanwhile, cook the rice according to the packet instructions. Stir the butter into the rice and set aside.

Sift the flour into a shallow bowl, then add the salt and pepper. Rinse the chicken thighs, shake off the excess water and then dip them into the seasoned flour, coating all sides thoroughly.

Heat the oil in a shallow frying pan over a medium heat. Once the oil is hot, fry the coated chicken thighs until golden brown.

Meanwhile, whisk the eggs, milk and nutmeg together, then stir this mixture into the cooked rice. Transfer it to a shallow baking dish that fits the chicken thighs laying side by side as closely as possible.

Once the chicken has browned, place it on top of the rice mixture and bake in the preheated oven for 45 minutes. Serve with a leafy green side salad and enjoy!

SARMA

Preparation time: 1-2 hours • Cooking time: 4+ hours
• Serves 4

1 head of sauerkraut or 2 x 1550g jars of rolled sauerkraut leaves (900g drained weight) • A little oil • 64g (½ cup) rice • 500g minced beef • 1 medium onion, finely chopped • Salt and black pepper • 125ml (½ cup) warm water • Smoked pancetta or other cured meat (optional) • Crème fraiche, to serve (optional) • Fresh parsley, to serve • For the sauce • 21g (1 tbsp) tomato pureé • 8g (1 level dessert spoon) flour • 2-5g (1-2 tsp) paprika • 1 vegetable stock cube • Boiling water

Wash the sauerkraut leaves thoroughly in cold water, then leave to drain before halving the larger leaves lengthways, cutting out the hard central vein. Smaller leaves can be used whole. Trim off any torn parts of the leaves. Brush the inside of a large saucepan with oil and lay any discarded sauerkraut in the bottom to prevent the sarmas from sticking.

Wash the rice until the water runs clear, then combine it with the minced beef, finely chopped onion, salt, pepper and warm water. Mix by hand for a few minutes until well combined.

Place a sauerkraut leaf on a clean surface, add a dessert spoonful of the filling near the edge closest to you and then roll up tightly. Tuck in the top and bottom ends to make a compact parcel, so that no filling is coming out. Place in the saucepan. Repeat this process until you run out of filling, placing the sarmas tightly next to each other in a circle. You may end up with more than one layer. Try to make them all approximately the same size (I like to make them about 3 by 8cm) for even cooking. If using, scatter some chopped pancetta or cured meat over the sarmas to give the dish a smoky flavour.

Place a small plate on top of the sarmas to keep them tightly packed during cooking. Pour boiling water into the saucepan until the sarmas and the plate are submerged. Bring to the boil and then simmer for 3 hours. Top up with boiling water from time to time to make sure the sarmas are always fully submerged.

Meanwhile, make the sauce. Mix the tomato purée with the flour and paprika in a bowl, gradually adding boiling water to make a paste. Crumble in the stock cube and then add enough water to make quite a runny mixture, resembling tomato juice. Tip this mixture into the saucepan and gently mix it with the rest of the liquid so that it penetrates through all the layers of sarma.

Simmer for another hour. Sarma gets better the longer it's cooked, and always tastes better on the second day. It's almost impossible to overcook it, you just need to make sure the water does not evaporate so keep topping up the liquid during cooking. When done, serve the sarma with some crème fraiche and chopped parsley.

Sarma (meaning wrapped in Turkish) is a popular dish in the former territories of the Ottoman Empire. It always uses some kind of a leaf (such as vine or cabbage) wrapped around a filling. In Bosnia, sarma is a typical winter dish, made using sauerkraut leaves wrapped around a meat, onion and rice filling. Each household used to pickle large barrels of cabbage in brine, which would provide vitamins, probiotics, fibre and minerals throughout the cold winter months, promoting good health and a strong immune system. Sarma always reminds me of New Years' Day, a perfect meal for the day after the night before.

I have attempted to provide exact measurements but our heritage recipes are always imprecise, relying on years of cooking experience. 'A pinch of this, a handful of that, a splash of the other. Mix until you get an even mixture, neither hard nor soft, bake until it's ready!' Cups are as close as you are going to get to precise measurements.

Sarma can be eaten on its own, although fresh bread or creamy mashed potatoes are really good accompaniments as they soak up the lovely tomato sauce perfectly. Sarma should be consumed within 3 days, but it freezes well too.

LYDIA'S CLAY POT CHICKEN

Preparation time: 45 minutes, plus 30 minutes to 1 hour for marinating • Cooking time: 45 minutes • Serves 4

500g chicken thigh fillets • 5cm fresh root ginger • 3 tbsp rice wine or Amontillado sherry • 1 tbsp sesame oil • 3 tbsp dark soy sauce • 1 tsp cornflour • 300ml boiling water • 8 dried shiitake mushrooms • 2 tbsp sunflower oil • ½ leek, finely sliced • 2 spring onions, halved lengthways and sliced into 2.5cm pieces • 3 shallots, sliced • 4 cloves of garlic, chopped • 225g tinned sliced bamboo shoots, drained • 300ml chicken stock or reserved shiitake soaking water • 1 tsp sugar • Salt and pepper

Born in Singapore (of Portuguese Eurasian heritage), my much-travelled mother Lydia Linford has lived in London for decades now. I was lucky enough to spend the years between the ages of four and eight living in Singapore: a formative experience, which I feel strongly contributed to my fascination with food. I have happy memories from that time of playing with my many cousins (my mother was one of six) and eating wonderful, varied food: ice kachang (a shaved ice dessert) after shopping at the Cold Storage Supermarket on Orchard Road, beautiful fresh mangosteens bought from sellers by the side of the road, Hainanese chicken rice enjoyed with my family at Swee Kee's and stick after stick of freshly grilled beef satay from the satay stalls by Singapore Harbour.

My mother's cooking as I grew up was open-minded, inventive and always tasty. When entertaining for family and friends she would go to great lengths, shopping days in advance for special ingredients and preparing a truly generous feast. I remember her taking me as a small child to shop in London's Chinatown and Soho's Italian delis, laying the foundation for my own food shopping habits. This Chinese-inspired recipe of hers is one I always enjoyed eating. The dried shiitake mushrooms – often called simply 'Chinese mushrooms' – are one of the ingredients she would stock up on when shopping in Chinatown. They bring a distinctive smoky flavour and satisfying chewy texture to the dish, so do be sure to use them.

Cut the chicken fillets into even chunks and place in a bowl. Cut the ginger in half, then peel and grate one of the pieces. Mix the grated ginger, rice wine, sesame oil, soy sauce and cornflour together. Add to the chicken, mixing well, then marinate in the fridge for 30 minutes to 1 hour.

Meanwhile, pour the boiling water over the shiitake mushrooms and set aside to soak for 25 minutes. Remove the softened mushrooms, cut off and discard the tough stems and halve the caps. If using the shiitake soaking water instead of chicken stock, strain and reserve it.

Preheat the oven to 180°c while you peel and slice the remaining ginger. Heat the oil in a wok or frying pan over a medium heat. When the oil is hot, add the sliced ginger, leek, spring onion, shallot and garlic and stir fry until fragrant. Add the marinated chicken pieces (reserving the marinade) and continue stir frying until they lose their raw colour on all sides. Add the shiitake mushrooms, bamboo shoots, reserved marinade, stock and sugar.

Bring the mixture to the boil and then transfer it to a Chinese clay pot or a casserole dish. Cover and cook in the preheated oven for 30 minutes. Taste and season with salt and pepper before serving with steamed rice and blanched or stir fried leafy greens, such as gai laan or bok choi.

LATOYAH MCALLISTER-JONES

Roti is the ultimate Guyanese dish for me. It was my favourite as a child and the one that makes me feel most connected to my grandmother and my Guyanese heritage. Roti was always a 'treat' as it takes a while to make and my nan worked long hours. When we had roti for dinner it was always on a Thursday, which is still my favourite day of the week!

Although I see roti as a very Guyanese dish, it is actually a traditional Indian flatbread introduced to Guyana by Indian indentured workers who arrived after the abolition of slavery. It speaks to the unique culture and history of Guyana, right at the top of the South American continent, but culturally more similar to the nearby Caribbean islands. Guyanese food is a mix of Chinese food (also brought by indentured workers) as well as Indian and African influences and cooking techniques.

During the first UK lockdown in spring 2020, I decided to perfect my roti game; I've always bought the shells from Caribbean shops when I visit London but hadn't made it myself in many, many years since being taught by my nan. Making roti gives me so much pleasure; it is a taste of childhood, of love and deep connection to my nan and our shared cultural heritage. My nan, Victorine McAllister, is my hero: an accomplished cook, baker, active community member and a published poet. She is a Guyanese woman through and through and I feel my most Guyanese when I make this dish!

I've also shared my favourite curry of hers, adjusted to reflect how I cook it with optional additions for that Guyanese twist. My nan usually put potatoes in her curries, which thicken the sauce and absorb lots of flavour. For best results, marinate the lamb overnight but it can be left for 3 or 4 hours if you're in a rush. This method can be replicated with any meat. Lamb can be fatty, which is where you get the flavour, but you can also spoon any excess fat out of the sauce along the way if there's too much oil. As with most things I learnt to cook from my nan, I never knew the exact measurements; you're just kind of guided by the spirit!

GUYANESE LAMB CURRY

Preparation time: 3-4 hours or overnight
• Cooking time: I hour • Serves 4

600g lamb shoulder, diced • 2-3 scotch bonnets • 3 cloves of garlic • 2 tbsp hot curry powder • ½ tbsp all-purpose seasoning • 1½ tsp ground cumin • 1½ tsp paprika • Salt and pepper • 3 tbsp vegetable oil • I medium onion • 3-4 fresh tomatoes • I vegetable stock cube • I tbsp tomato purée • I medium potato (optional) • ½ a green mango or I green apple (optional)

Wash and dry the diced lamb. Deseed I of the scotch bonnets, peel I of the garlic cloves and then finely chop them both. Combine the chilli and garlic with the hot curry powder, all-purpose seasoning, ground cumin, paprika and I tablespoon of the oil. Add salt and ground black pepper to taste, then rub the mixture thoroughly into the meat and store in the fridge overnight.

The next day, chop the remaining scotch bonnets, garlic and onion. Fry in a large pot on a medium heat with the remaining oil until soft. Add the meat and continue frying until browned and coated in the onion mixture. Finely chop or blend the fresh tomatoes and then add them to the pot.

Pour in enough water to cover the meat, crumble in stock cube, bring to the boil and then simmer for 30 to 40 minutes. Taste the sauce and adjust the seasoning to suit your personal tastes. If using, dice the potato and green mango or apple, then add to the curry. Stir in the tomato purée (this will thicken the sauce slightly) and then simmer the curry for a further 5 to 10 minutes. Serve with my Guyanese roti and eat with your hands!

LATOYAH MCALLISTER-JONES

MY GRANDMOTHER'S GUYANESE ROTI

Preparation time: 45 minutes, plus 1 hour resting • Cooking time: 5 minutes • Makes 6

272g plain flour • 136g self-raising flour • 1½ tsp salt • 68ml cold water • 20g salted butter • 45ml olive or vegetable oil • If preferred, replace the fats above with ghee or shortening

Stage 1
Sift and mix the flours together in a bowl, then add the salt. Slowly pour the cold water into the bowl and work the mixture into a soft but slightly tacky dough. Don't overwork your dough otherwise it will become too stiff. Cover with a wet tea towel or kitchen roll to prevent a crust forming and rest for 30 minutes.

Stage 2
Once rested, your dough should look smooth and have slightly expanded. Roll it into a long, thick cylinder and then cut into 6 portions (about a handful of dough each).

Warm the salted butter and olive oil together for 30 seconds in the microwave. Cut out a square of greaseproof paper and set aside.

Flour your work surface and one of your dough balls, then roll it into a thin round. Use the greaseproof paper to dab the melted fats across the surface of the dough. With a sharp knife, cut a straight line in the dough from the centre of the circle to the edge. Starting from the cut, carefully roll the circle into a cone shape, tucking in the end.

Repeat this process with the remaining dough balls, then rest the greased and folded cones in a bowl covered with a wet tea towel or kitchen roll for 30 to 45 minutes.

Stage 3
Heat a flat skillet or frying pan on a medium heat and flour the work surface. Prepare a place to rest the cooked roti, a large round plate, a clean tea towel, a layer of tin foil and a layer of greaseproof paper. Make sure the foil and paper are big enough to wrap the breads in.

Roll each cone of dough out once to a thin round. Carefully place the round into the centre of the hot skillet or frying pan and cook for 2 minutes on each side. Use the greaseproof paper to add a layer of the butter and oil mixture to each side of the roti, using short dabbing movements.

When lightly browned on each side, place the cooked roti on the plate. Before you wrap it up, hold the roti between the palms of your hands, lift a little and clap. Repeat this action 2 or 3 times to release the layers in your roti. Repeat the whole rolling and cooking process with the remaining dough, then serve the roti with dhal or curry and eat with your fingers!

LUCIO'S BRAZILIAN CARNE DE PANELA

Much is said about food being a lot more than just food; it makes up a big chunk of our memories and our stories. We often talk about food smells that take us back in time, or dishes that place us right back at home, visiting a relative or at school.

For me, one of the dishes that takes me right back in time is carne de panela (meat cooked in a pan) with pasta. It is a simple and easy dish but it was something special for us in the family, as it was one of my maternal grandmother's Sunday lunch signature dishes which she passed on to her daughters, including my mother (although they all added their own twists to it).

As three out of her four children live abroad, including myself, carne de panela also regularly featured on the food wish list we would share with our mother ahead of any visit to see her in Brazil. It also became a favourite for my UK-born children.

But the dish now has an even more special meaning to me. In 2019, my mother was diagnosed with terminal cancer and I spent as much time as possible with her during that year, together with my siblings, to support her and be with her for the time she had left with us. A brutal realisation that things would not be the same ever again came with the fact that, for the first time, my trip to Brazil did not include the usual advance food wish list. This was the time for us to feed her, not the other way round.

During a rare week when she was feeling slightly better, we decided to make carne de panela, with her instructing us on what to do and helping as much as possible with the prep work. For a brief moment, Dona Vania (as we tended to call her) was back with us as the fantastic (if not sometimes electric) cook she was, and through a dish that meant so much to all of us.

As the one who inherited her interest in cooking, and the same disregard for detailed recipes, it was a sad but proud moment to prepare this dish for her. It was also the one I chose to make for my family in the UK when we joined my brother and my sisters via Zoom this past Boxing Day to mark the first year since her death.

That was because, for me, carne de panela will never be a simple but tasty dish. It will always be one of the quickest ways to travel back in time and place with the family to be at my mother's or my grandmother's kitchen whenever I desperately long for those childhood days.

As mentioned, my mother was one of those cooks who didn't keep or follow detailed recipes, irrespective of whether the dishes were regular ones or invented on the spot, depending on what was in the cupboard or the fridge. Always a problem as she could never precisely replicate any of her dishes! This also applied to carne de panela, so take the recipe I've shared as a reference point and feel free to adjust or change ingredients as much as you want: that was the 'Dona Vania' way!

BRAZILIAN CARNE DE PANELA

This dish can be served just with pasta, or with a salad as well (my grandmother's favourite side dish was another good lump of carbs in the shape of a potato and vegetable mayonnaise salad). Many people in Brazil eat pasta dishes accompanied by pinto beans or similar.

Preparation time: 12 hours • Cooking time: 2-3 hours • Serves 4

---

1 whole piece of topside beef, or any roasting joint • 150ml red wine vinegar • 1 tsp salt • Pinch of ground black pepper • 2 onions, roughly chopped • 3 cloves of garlic, crushed • 1 red or green pepper, sliced • Vegetable oil • 500g pasta (ideally tagliatelle or any other flat type) • Parmesan cheese (optional)

Preferably a day in advance, pierce the beef joint liberally with a small knife or scissors to help the meat absorb the seasoning. Mix the vinegar, salt, pepper, roughly chopped onions, crushed garlic and sliced pepper together, then coat the meat with the mixture. Let the beef rest in the marinade for at least 12 hours or, ideally, overnight.

Reserve the remaining marinade. Heat a pan with a small amount of oil and seal the beef joint. The aim here is to let the meat burn a bit on the pan as that will add a deeper flavour to the sauce. The longer you leave it to seal, the darker the sauce will be.

Once well sealed, add the marinade to the pan, cover with a lid, bring it to the boil and then gently simmer, adding water as needed to keep the beef about half covered in liquid while cooking. Keep cooking for at least 2 to 3 hours, checking often to make sure the pan isn't dry and to see if the meat is soft. Check the sauce for seasoning and adjust to taste; add more sliced pepper and/or onions to the sauce if you want more texture.

You can prepare the meat a day in advance, reheating it and reducing the sauce (if needed) closer to serving time. When ready to serve, cook the pasta and drain it. Transfer the pasta to a deep serving dish, pour in most of the sauce from the meat pan and mix. Slice the beef joint, place the slices on top of the pasta then pour the remaining sauce on top. It's now ready to serve, topped with some freshly grated parmesan if you like.

My mother is a natural cook with a phenomenal instinct for flavours and timings. I admire her ability to improvise and entertain at the drop of a hat. I grew up helping her in the kitchen, preparing food for our huge family. My father loved good food and bold flavour combinations like ham croquettes dipped in sugar, or chorizo and chocolate. He taught me the importance of fresh produce and a strong pantry. I still love cooking with my mother and even when I am not with her, I am never cooking alone, as I find that the kitchen evokes the smells, sounds and conversations of my childhood. Certain dishes mark traditions in our house; they are rituals that remind me who I am and bring me home.

When I moved from Spain to Bristol, I fell in love with the city's diverse culinary culture. The food scene is vibrant and ever-changing, with so many interesting restaurants, cafés, delis and food shops where you can eat and get inspiration. The farmers' markets have become the highlight of my Saturdays. There, I always meet interesting people and find new exotic ingredients to cook with. My desire to experiment with new foods has by no means diminished my appreciation for Spanish cuisine; rather, it has brought into focus the dishes that I simply cannot give up, those that I come back to time and time again. Through Spanish food, I share my culture, and through the myriad foods I try in Bristol, I learn about others' cultures. It is a privilege to live in such a diverse, foodie city.

SPANISH CHICKEN FABADA

This is a warming dish full of Spanish flavour. It can be adapted to whatever ingredients you have available (such as chickpeas instead of butter beans, capers instead of olives) and the key is the time they spend together. Therefore, it tastes even better the day after it's cooked or can be prepared a day or two in advance and kept in the fridge until you are ready to cook.

Preparation time: 25 minutes
• Cooking time: I hour 30 minutes • Serves 4

4-6 chicken thighs • Salt and pepper, to taste • ¼ tsp sweet paprika • 400g tinned butter beans in water • 200g spicy cooking chorizo (chorizo picante) • I sweet red chilli • 150g fresh cherry tomatoes • I large red onion, sliced • 2 red Romano peppers, sliced • 400g tinned cherry or plum tomatoes (or 400g passata) • I00g black olives (pitted if you prefer) • I tbsp green or black tapenade (optional) • I bay leaf • 2 sprigs of thyme • I tsp sugar • Good quality olive oil • I tbsp chopped flat leaf parsley

Preheat the oven to 175°c (Gas Mark 4). It's up to you whether to leave the skin on the chicken thighs and take them off the bone or not. Season the chicken thighs with salt and pepper and put them in a heavy-based casserole dish, preferably one that has a lid. Next, sprinkle the sweet paprika over the chicken to get an even coating. Drain the butter beans and add them to the casserole dish.

Take the skin off the chorizo (use a small knife to nick the skin and then pull it back) and cut into 0.5cm slices. Run a small knife along the side of the chilli, making a score line in it, but leaving it whole. Wash and dry the fresh cherry tomatoes and add them to the casserole dish whole, along with the sliced chorizo, whole chilli, onion and peppers. Next, add the tinned tomatoes (or passata) along with the olives, tapenade and herbs.

Sprinkle the sugar over the casserole contents and season well with salt and pepper. Pour a generous amount of good olive oil over the top and put the lid on the dish, or cover tightly with foil.

Transfer it to the preheated oven and cook for I hour and 30 minutes.

Just before serving, sprinkle the freshly chopped flat leaf parsley over the dish. Serve it with your favourite bread.

MOHINDER AND SUNIL'S MAGICAL GREEN CHICKEN

This is a recipe which Mohinder made regularly for us. It has a Singaporean touch with the use of curry powder. If preferred, you can use chicken thighs and drumsticks instead of the whole birds. Sunil loved to cook this dish too.

Preparation time: 25 minutes • Cooking time: 1 hour • Serves 6

1 large bunch of fresh coriander • 5 bunches of spring onions, green parts only • 6 tbsp ghee • 2 tbsp cumin seeds • 6 cloves of garlic, finely chopped • 2.5cm (1 inch) fresh ginger, grated • 3-4 hot green chillies, finely chopped (or more to taste) • 2 medium chickens, skinned and cut into small pieces • 1 tsp curry powder • ½ tsp chilli powder • ½ tsp garam masala • ½ tsp salt • 2 medium potatoes, peeled and quartered

Wash the coriander and roughly chop the leaves and stems. Roughly blitz the coriander (both leaves and stems) with the spring onions in a blender.

Heat the ghee in a pan and when hot, add the cumin seeds. Reduce the heat to medium. When the seeds sizzle, put the onion and coriander paste into the pan with the garlic, ginger and chillies. Mix for 2 minutes and then add the chicken pieces.

After 1 to 2 minutes, add all the spices and salt to taste. Turn everything in the pan to coat the chicken. Cook for 5 minutes until the chicken is coloured and then reduce the heat. Put in the potatoes, give them a stir and then add enough hot water to almost cover the chicken.

Bring to the boil and then turn down to a simmer. Cook for around 25 to 30 minutes until the potatoes are soft. Serve with rice or rotis.

My sister Mohinder's kindness and big heart showed in everything she did. She always had a warm smile for everyone and a plate of food ready to welcome you to her home, and even packed pots of snacks and hot food to sustain you on your journey home (no matter how long or short our journey home was). She was known as Mohinder massi (very respected aunty) to everyone and her cooking was almost heavenly. She took our everyday staples – dal, gobi aloo (cauliflower and potatoes), parathas, rice – and somehow transformed them into mouth-watering dishes.

She married into an Indian family who had lived for generations in Singapore. Singapore has a close relationship to India, as both during and after the Empire and after World War Two, South Indian workers travelled there for work to help rebuild Singapore. When they made the journey to England (once again to help where workers were required) they brought the influence of Singaporean foods with them. Mohinder took those recipes and with her natural culinary flair, made them her own. My abiding memory is of her coming on the train from Kent to London with bags of containers filled with freshly made food for us. I'm sure everyone on the train must have got hungry from the smell!

No matter how carefully we watched her cook, none of us could recreate her dishes and make them taste like hers. She had a magic touch in her hands. Thankfully she transferred her love of cooking to her son Sunil and after she passed away, he carried on making those dishes for us all to enjoy. With his big-hearted kindness, thoughtfulness and generosity he would say to us: "let me cook whatever you want to eat – let me cook all your favourites," and he would cook with effortless joy for his family and friends. Sadly, Sunil passed away too in 2021 and we will always cherish him and his mum through the memories of the gorgeous dishes they both used to cook for us.

I was born and brought up in Goa, which is one of the most beautiful states on the west coast of India. Goa has many traditions and a cuisine that have been heavily influenced by Portuguese culture, since Goa was a Portuguese colony until 1961.

Pork vindalho was one of the many dishes introduced to Goa around 1510 by Portuguese explorers who travelled with their garlic-flavoured vinegar stew called 'carne de vinha d'alhos' which literally means meat marinated or cooked in wine and garlic. The dish was then tweaked to meet the local tastes and since there was no wine vinegar available in Goa at that time, it was substituted with the locally produced palm vinegar.

This is a very nostalgic dish for me, as it played a very festive part in cultural and social gatherings for the Goan catholic community, featuring on the menu of any special occasions that were celebrated from the feast of the village's patron saint to weddings.

St. Estevam, where I grew up, is a very scenic village and there were always great cooks making their own version of this dish that would fill me up with joy as the aroma filled the air during the December festivities. My mom has always been a great cook and an influencer; her food was and still is very much enjoyed by the family. I used to get to see the whole vindalho making process, right from the pig getting slaughtered by the local butcher to how it was all cooked. There is a story to tell even though pork vindalho is a very simple dish that uses spices to bring out the best flavour in the meat. The result when it's all put together is what makes pork vindalho a very special dish on my list of food that I would also like my children to know about and learn to cook, continuing the tradition of enjoying a very good vindalho.

RYAN'S GOAN PORK

Preparation time: 30 minutes, plus 2 hours marinating
• Cooking time: 1 hour • Serves 6-8

1kg fatty pork, cubed • 4 medium onions, finely diced • 4 cloves of garlic, finely diced • 2.5cm (1 inch) fresh ginger, finely diced • Salt, sugar and vinegar to taste

For the paste • 15 dried red chillies, halved and deseeded • 2.5cm (1 inch) fresh ginger • 1 clove of garlic • 2.5cm (1 inch) cinnamon stick • 2 tsp cumin seeds • 1 tsp ground turmeric • ½ tsp peppercorns • ¼ tsp cloves • 250-300ml red wine vinegar

Season the cubed pork with salt and set aside while you make the paste. Put all the ingredients into a mortar and grind with a pestle, or use a blender to blitz them. Use the smaller quantity of red wine vinegar first, adding more if needed to get the right consistency and flavour. Marinate the meat in the spice paste for 2 hours or overnight in the fridge.

Heat a little oil in a heavy-based pan, then add the finely diced onions, garlic and ginger. Sauté until the onion is translucent, then add the marinated pork and leave to cook on a low heat for 10 minutes, stirring occasionally.

Add enough warm water to cover the pork and continue to cook on a low heat, stirring at regular intervals. When the volume of liquid has reduced by half, season the vindalho with salt, sugar and vinegar to taste. Once the meat is tender, serve with rice or Goan steamed rice cakes (sannas).

Chickpeas are a much relied upon lunchtime staple in street markets and cafés across India, usually served with puffed fried breads and pickle on the side. There are regional differences in how the masala is prepared. In South India, coconut, curry leaves and mustard seeds reflect taste preferences, but it is the Punjabi version which is widely acclaimed for its tart-sour flavours and onion-ginger-tomato masala. The dried seeds of sour pomegranates, known as anardana, are an important seasoning. The seeds are pounded and added at the end of cooking to impart a fresh-tasting tartness. The dried sticky pomegranate seeds have a fruity, molasses-like flavour, but they're a beast to grind to a powder in an electric grinder or with a mortar and pestle and have a gritty texture. However, they are brilliant when boiled and the resulting cooking liquor is strained into masalas. Although the ready-ground seeds aren't quite as flavoursome, they are a sight easier to use in recipes. Don't limit yourself to sprinkling anardana into chana masala: try it in salad dressings, over French fries and on roasted root vegetables.

ROOPA'S PUNJABI CHANAS

When buying dried chickpeas, look for the larger beige variety known as Kabuli chanas. If you can't get hold of ground pomegranate, use mango powder (amchoor) instead. This dish benefits from being made 1 or 2 days beforehand so the flavours can develop.

Preparation time: 20 minutes, plus optional overnight soaking • Cooking time: 1 hour • Serves 4-6

150g dried chickpeas or 400g tinned chickpeas • 50g ghee or 4-6 tbsp sunflower oil • 1 large onion, diced • 50g fresh ginger, peeled and finely chopped • ¾ tsp ground turmeric • ¾ tsp garam masala • ½ tsp Kashmiri chilli powder • 400g tinned chopped tomatoes • 2 tsp pomegranate powder (anardana) • Lime wedges, to serve

If using dried chickpeas, soak them overnight in cold water with ¼ teaspoon bicarbonate of soda. Drain the soaked chickpeas and rinse under running water. Put them in a pressure cooker and cover generously with water, about three times the volume. Cook under pressure for 30 to 40 minutes, or until they are completely tender, and then turn off the heat. Once the pressure has been released, mash some of the chickpeas against the sides of the pan. If you are using tinned chickpeas, simply drain off the liquid and rinse them under running water.

Heat the ghee or oil in a casserole over a medium heat. Add the onion and fry until golden. Stir in the ginger, turmeric, garam masala, and chilli powder and cook for another 30 seconds. Add the tomatoes and cook the masala, stirring all the time, until it has thickened. This should take about 10 minutes.

Stir the chickpeas and their cooking water into the masala, or if you are using tinned chickpeas add them to the pan with about 300ml of fresh water. Simmer for about 10 to 15 minutes, adding more hot water if it becomes too thick. Stir in enough pomegranate powder to give the masala a fruity and tart flavour. Serve with lime wedges on the side and North Indian bread, such as puri and chapatis.

SIMON MACDONNELL

MY MOTHER'S FISH PIE

This was always such a lovely treat to have on a cold evening for a warming supper. Best served with peas, broccoli or buttered spinach. You can swap the haddock with any chunky white fish, such as hake, cod or even monkfish if you are feeling generous.

Preparation time: 45 minutes • Cooking time: 30 minutes • Serves 6-8

For the filling • 300ml milk • 100ml double cream • 500g undyed smoked haddock • 500g salmon fillets • 250g shelled king prawns • 2 leeks • 2 sprigs of fresh thyme • 50g butter • 30g flour • 1 glass of white wine • 1 tbsp Dijon mustard • 4 sprigs of fresh tarragon • 2 lemons, zested • Salt and pepper

For the topping • 2kg Maris Piper or King Edward potatoes • 200ml milk • 100g butter

For the filling

Heat the milk and cream in a heavy-based pan until hot but not boiling. Add the fish (but not the prawns) and slowly poach until barely cooked. Strain the poaching liquid and set aside. Do not throw this away!

Meanwhile, finely chop the leeks and thyme leaves, then sweat them in the butter until soft. Add the flour and cook on a low heat until you have a paste. Pour in the wine and allow it to reduce on a low heat, then add the reserved poaching liquid to the pan. Let the mixture thicken over a low heat for 5 minutes but do not boil.

Add the mustard, tarragon and lemon zest to the sauce, then season it with lots of black pepper and some salt (but not too much if using smoked haddock, as this is already salty). Gently fold the poached fish and the prawns into the sauce, then take the pan off the heat. Make sure you are happy with the taste and do feel free to play around with extras of your choice as everyone has personal favourites. Try a dash of Tabasco or some anchovies, fresh parsley, spinach, peas or even soft-boiled eggs, for example.

For the topping

Peel the potatoes or leave the skins on according to your preference. Cook them in a large pan of boiling water until tender, then drain and let them steam dry a little. Heat the milk and butter together, then pour them into the cooked potatoes while whisking with a fork to make a light and fluffy mash. Season with salt and pepper. I add Dijon mustard too, as I love mustard in my fish pie!

Spoon the filling into a ceramic baking dish and pipe the mash over the top. Bake the fish pie in a preheated oven at 200°c for 30 minutes, until nicely browned and crispy on top.

My mum sadly passed away 5 years ago but she was such an amazing, creative cook. She gave me the inspiration which meant I became hooked on cooking and was later to pursue it as a career.

She largely followed her instincts when it came to cooking and recipes were generally off the cuff and from the heart. She grew fruit and vegetables for much of the year and her garden gave her most of the ingredients that she used to create her culinary delights.

This fish pie is just one of many recipes which I have written down from memories of watching her in the kitchen all those years ago. I remember it was a real treat on a Saturday or Sunday and one of those family suppers that warms a winter's night and yet is also a lovely summery meal with seasonal vegetables or a garden salad.

PINDA'S BATTERED VEAL ESCALOPES

I grew up with a famous dad. You see, he was a footballer when football wasn't about the money but you played for the love of the game. So he had fame but not fortune. Everywhere he went he was recognised, with people approaching him and saying "Hey Pinda, the legend, how are you, c'mon let's have a drink!" followed by various stories starting with "Do you remember…." Those were good days.

My dad loved life and he lived it to the full. And he loved food. It was nothing for him to jump in the car and drive 100 miles to get to the place that served the best lamb on a spit. He never believed in vegetarianism when I was growing up. Vegetables, if added to a meal, would have to be well seasoned and freshly prepared. He was never fond of leftovers either. The centrepiece of every meal would have to be meat, and lots of it. He loved them all, from lamb and pork all the way to veal, which was and still is a go-to meat in Bosnia and Herzegovina (and beyond).

He wasn't a versatile cook, but what he did cook was absolutely delicious and had to be made with the best ingredients. One of his signature dishes that he mastered to perfection was battered veal escalopes, served with whatever happened to be around vegetable-wise (usually season-dependant, so in spring/summer it would be creamed spinach and colder months would call for podvarak: thinly sliced sour cabbage, similar to sauerkraut, braised with pancetta) and almost always 'restovani krompir' (potatoes sautéed with onions).

I am giving you a recipe for both the battered veal escalopes and the potato side in the hope that you will enjoy it as much as I used to and still immensely do. Every time I make this dish it

takes me back to my childhood, Dad coming home from shopping in the morning with a big piece of veal that he himself cut thinly into perfect escalopes, whacking each one with a meat tenderiser so they were thin and soft when cooked, then salted and stacked up on top of each other, and mixing the batter just to ensure it sticks to the meat perfectly. I can smell the freshly cut meat, the batter, potatoes cooking, onions frying… I can still hear all those noises, too, as well as him calling me to provide last minute help with finding that dish he was looking for but couldn't see even though it was right before his eyes. Happy days. Carefree days.

Those are happy memories but also very sad too. I miss him terribly, his presence, our laughs (we were so very similar), cappuccinos in a café just outside our block of flats where he would almost religiously wait for me to come home from work. I remember him sitting there with two cappuccinos waiting and then we would sit there together, chatting and putting the world right. Oh, how I miss those days! And how I long to hug him again!

I'd also like to share with you a very special recipe for what we mainly call kitnikez, also known as kotunjata, sir od jabuka or 'apple cheese', which you can find on page 166. This is usually made with quinces, but apples can also be used. As my apple tree produced an abundance of apples this year, I had to make a batch. The recipe is dedicated to my grandma Emma (Emilia) who used to make this when I was little. Every time I make this delight it takes me back to those carefree times and I think of her. I'm hoping that old traditional recipes like these will be saved and not forgotten.

OUR CELEBRATED PINDA'S BATTERED VEAL ESCALOPES WITH SAUTÉED POTATOES

I really hope that you will give this recipe a go. It's easy and simple and sometimes, that is what we need. We use veal but you can easily swap it for chicken, pork or even thinly sliced aubergine (my dad loved aubergines done this way too… served with some other meat, of course!).

Preparation time: 20 minutes • Cooking time: 20 minutes • Serves 4

For the battered escalopes • 500g veal escalopes, tenderised • 1 egg • 200ml milk • Salt and pepper • Plain flour • Oil, for frying

For the sautéed potatoes • 800g potatoes • 3-4 tbsp oil • 2 onions, sliced • Black pepper • Powdered bouillon (or ½ a stock cube)

For the battered escalopes

Tenderising and seasoning the meat with salt then leaving it to rest is the key to really tasty escalopes. The same rules apply to any other meat, not just veal. Cut the escalopes to your desired size and sprinkle with salt on each side. Stack them up and leave to rest for 15 to 20 minutes.

Beat the egg and milk together, then whisk in the seasoning and gradually add enough flour to make a thick, pancake-like batter. Leave to rest.

Heat the oil in a frying pan, making sure it is at least 1 cm deep. When hot, dip the escalopes in the batter and carefully lay them into the oil. Fry on a medium heat for 1 to 2 minutes on each side. Drain on kitchen paper and keep warm until you're ready to serve.

Fry any leftover batter like thin crumpets; they are delicious on their own or with some feta and eggs, if they last until the morning.

For the sautéed potatoes

Peel and cube the potatoes, then cook them in boiling water until just done. Drain thoroughly. Meanwhile, heat the oil in a pan and add the sliced onions. Fry on a medium heat for 10 minutes until they start to brown slightly. Stir in the bouillon or stock cube along with lots of black pepper.

Add the boiled potatoes to the pan, mix well and fry together for 5 minutes. The potatoes shouldn't be dry, so if they are, add another 1 or 2 tablespoons of oil. Serve the restovani krompir (sautéed potatoes and onions) alongside the hot battered escalopes.

RIZ BEL BAZELA (RICE AND PEAS) – A SYRIAN RECIPE BY SUSAN ARAFEH

Preparation time: 15 minutes, plus 1 hour for soaking • Cooking time: 30-40 minutes • Serves 4

200g Arborio or basmati rice • ½ tsp salt • 200g minced meat • 3 tbsp vegetable oil or 2 tbsp ghee • Salt and black pepper • 3 medium carrots • 1 big handful of peas, shelled or frozen • Pine nuts and flaked almonds (optional)

Cover the rice in boiling water, add the half teaspoon of salt and leave to soak for 1 hour. Meanwhile, fry the minced meat in a little of the vegetable oil or ghee until it is well cooked and no longer watery. Season to taste with salt and black pepper, then set aside.

Drain the soaked rice and rinse until the water runs clear. Peel and dice the carrots, then fry them in a teaspoon of oil until tender. Combine the carrots, peas and some black pepper with the washed rice in a pan. Add a cup of hot water to the mixture and cook for 10 minutes on a medium heat. Add a couple of extra spoonfuls of water, turn the heat down low and continue to simmer until the rice is cooked and the water has evaporated.

To serve as an individual portion, take a small bowl and put a sprinkling of pine nuts and flaked almonds in the bottom. Then add a layer of mince followed by a layer of the cooked rice and pea mixture. Gently press down and cover with a plate. Hold the bowl and plate together and quickly turn them upside down. Leave it for 1 minute to settle and then remove the bowl.

You can also serve this with the traditional salad of tomatoes, cucumber, parsley, lemon, garlic and a pinch of dried mint, or some yoghurt with cucumber and mint on the side. I hope you enjoy eating it.

Cooking plays an important role in Syrian culture, no matter where you are from – the city, the suburbs or the remote villages – and whether you are highly educated or just able to read the alphabet. Cooking is a very important component of everyday life and is a key topic of discussion among women.

Because women in Syria think a lot about cooking, the first question to be posed after saying good morning is usually: "what are we going to eat today?" Therefore, most men try to avoid this question by asking: "what vegetables and groceries do you want me to buy from the shop today?"

Nowadays, the rhythm of life has changed. Most women are working so to think of something tasty and quick to cook is the solution. Everyone – men, women and children alike – agrees on rice and peas as the perfect answer because it is easy to cook and very tasty. You can make it simple, so that the average family can afford it, or you can add a lot of meat, pine nuts, cashews and almonds to make it more indulgent for those who can afford more ingredients. It is the number one everyday meal and can be served as a rice dish or wrapped in filo pastry as a parcel with yoghurt on the side.

There is also something funny about rice and peas. When a mother is looking for a bride for her son, she will ask: "do you have rice and peas?" which refers to white skin, fair hair and green eyes. This is because an Arab mother's preference is for her son's bride to have these attributes which are highly desirable features in the Middle East.

In short, rice and peas is the number one preference for Syrian families. To understand what I am talking about, you will have to try it and judge for yourself… I'm ready to invite you whenever you want. Bon Appetit!

CANDI'S JOLLOF RICE AND SALMON

Photo: @JonCraig_Photos

Isn't it strange how you forget so many details in life but there are some moments you remember so clearly? That's exactly how I feel about my first experience of jollof rice. I remember it like it was yesterday: the huge silver pan, the billowing smoke wafting over a gorgeously spiced aroma, the sweet scent of plantain in the background.

I couldn't have been more than 11 years old the first time I had jollof rice. For many people of African descent, that'll seem very late to the party but having grown up in a wonderful foster family, it wasn't until the latter half of my childhood that I started spending time with my biological family.

I'd travelled up to London to spend time with Dad and his family and I vividly remember the eating experience. I was sitting in the bustling living room when I was handed a plate of food with a hearty mound of rice that shone with red and yellow colours. I tucked in, nervous about this unfamiliar but gorgeous-smelling treat, and after the first mouthful, I was sold.

Two decades on and jollof rice is still one of my all-time favourite dishes. It brings such fond memories: the sound of loud, contagious laughter in Nigerian family living rooms, the heart-warming feeling of colourful celebrations, family bonds and all ages uniting over food.

For this recipe, I'm bringing together two of my favourite foods from both cultures of my upbringing. I've paired my take on jollof rice with salmon, my favourite fish and an ode to growing up by the sea in a big family. My late foster Mum, the most wonderful person to ever walk this earth, would treat me to the most delicious salmon dinners. I worked two jobs as a teenager and I'd always come home to a plate waiting after a long day at work. It became my ultimate comfort food and I think of my darling mother so fondly when I remember this.

CANDI'S JOLLOF RICE AND SALMON

Please enjoy my jollof rice and salmon recipe. It's far from official, but it's mine and one that's very close to my heart. I hope it brings you some of the comfort that it has given me over the years.

Preparation time: 20 minutes • Cooking time: 1 hour 15 minutes • Serves 4 (with leftovers)

400g tinned plum tomatoes • 2 bell peppers, deseeded • 1-2 scotch bonnet peppers (depending on how much spice you like) • 2 onions, roughly chopped • A drizzle of sunflower, vegetable or olive oil • 1 tbsp tomato paste • 1 tbsp grated ginger • 1 tbsp grated garlic • 2 bay leaves • 500g long grain rice • 400ml chicken stock • For the spice blend • 1 tbsp each thyme, curry powder and all-purpose seasoning • 1 tsp each salt and white pepper • ½ tbsp cayenne pepper

For the salmon • 4 salmon fillets • ½ lemon • Salt and pepper • Fresh parsley, roughly chopped

Firstly, make your sauce. Blend the tinned tomatoes, peppers, scotch bonnets and one of the onions together until the mixture is lovely and smooth. Pop this to one side – you'll need it later.

Next, heat up the oil in a large pot or wok and fry the remaining onion for 3 to 5 minutes or until it turns translucent. Stir in the tomato paste, ginger and garlic to continue frying for 5 minutes until it all blends together. Be careful that none of this catches and burns.

Pour the scotch bonnet sauce into the pan and let it heat up, then add the bay leaves and spice blend. You can either get a jollof seasoning mix from your local African food store (a great excuse to visit) or make your own using the spices in the ingredients list. You'll want to give this mixture a good fry on a lower heat for around 20 to 30 minutes. Keep stirring often so it doesn't burn.

While you're cooking the sauce, wash the rice well in a sieve until the water runs clear. Parboil it for no longer than 5 minutes, then add it to the pan of sauce. Stir to coat the rice well with the sauce and then add the chicken stock. Taste to check the flavour and season if needed.

Give the rice a stir and then cover the pan with a lid. Leave it for 30 minutes on a low-medium heat but keep checking back to make sure it has enough liquid and doesn't burn.

While the rice is cooking in the sauce, prepare the salmon. Preheat the oven to 180°c and place the salmon fillets on a baking tray. Squeeze the lemon over the salmon, then season it with salt, pepper and fresh parsley. Drizzle lightly with oil and cook in the preheated oven for around 12 minutes.

Give the rice a good stir and make sure it has absorbed the liquid fully, then turn off the heat and let it stand for 5 to 10 minutes. Serve a hearty mound of jollof rice with a fillet of salmon per person and salad or vegetables of your choice on the side. The beauty of jollof is that it's super versatile so you can keep making it and serving it with whatever you like.

My mother's family originates from Aleppo in Syria. My grandparents left in 1910 for economic reasons and settled in Egypt as it had become the new El Dorado, due to the opening of the Suez Canal in 1869. The Jews of Aleppo had developed an elite cooking style which featured fine ingredients such as cinnamon and allspice, and exotic flavours such as tamarind paste and pomegranate molasses. Dried fruits were commonly available in the markets of Aleppo and were added to all sorts of vegetable and meat dishes. This remained very much my grandmother's style of cooking. She taught my mother everything she knew, and I have tried to keep the tradition going in my own way.

I have shared two Syrian Jewish recipes for this book: layered beef stew (opposite) and borekas, which you can find on page 142. These little pies are the trademark and the pride of Jews of Spanish descent. Their ancestors were expelled from Spain in 1492 and most of them settled in the Ottoman Empire and the Balkans. My father's family moved from there to Egypt just before the First World War as the Ottoman Empire had by then disintegrated. Borekas were a staple in my family and part of my childhood. Every housewife had her own variation and prided herself that hers were the best. The ones I remember most fondly are my mother's as her pastry just melted in the mouth.

LAH'MEH FIL MEH'LEH
(LAYERED SWEET AND SOUR BEEF STEW)

This Syrian Jewish dish favours the sweet and sour combination of ingredients. It's very easy to prepare, as it's all cooked in one pot. The flavour will improve if prepared a day ahead and reheated in the oven before serving.

Preparation time: 30 minutes • Cooking time: 2+ hours • Serves 6-8

900g stewing beef • 2½ tsp salt • ¼ tsp black pepper • ½ tsp ground cinnamon • 1½ tsp allspice • 2 medium onions • 2 medium potatoes • 1 large sweet potato • 1 medium aubergine • 3 tbsp vegetable oil • ¾ cup (134g) pitted prunes • 400g tinned chopped tomatoes • 2½ cups (625ml) water • 3 heaped tbsp tomato paste • Juice of 2 lemons + 3 tbsp • 1 tbsp Worcestershire sauce or pomegranate molasses • 1 tbsp tamarind paste • ¼ cup (51g) firmly packed dark brown sugar • ¼ tsp salt

First, prepare the layers. Cube the stewing beef and then combine it with the salt, pepper, cinnamon and allspice in a bowl, mixing well with your hands. Cut the onions into wedges and separate them into layers, then peel and chop both types of potato into medium chunks. Cut the aubergine into 2cm cubes.

Pour the vegetable oil into a heatproof casserole dish. Spread half the onions in a single layer over the oil. Place half the meat over the onions, pressing down firmly. If using a large saucepan, you may have to use all the onions in one layer and then all the meat. Add the vegetables in layers, beginning with the white potatoes, followed by the sweet potatoes, prunes and then aubergines, in that order. Press down firmly and then pour the chopped tomatoes over the vegetables.

Next, prepare the sauce. In a medium saucepan, combine the water, tomato paste, lemon juice, Worcestershire sauce or molasses, tamarind paste, dark brown sugar and salt. Give the mixture a stir, quickly bring it to the boil and then pour the sauce over the layers in the casserole dish.

Cover with a lid and simmer the stew over a low heat for 1 hour. Correct the seasoning to taste. You may have to add more brown sugar, as the sauce should have a sweet-tart taste. Preheat the oven to 180°c (Gas Mark 4) and then transfer the casserole dish to the oven and cook for another 1 hour 30 minutes, or up to 2 hours until the potatoes and aubergines are soft. If necessary, cook uncovered for a further 15 minutes if the sauce needs to be reduced. Serve with white rice.

SHARING OUR ...
SNACKS & DRINKS

"My children help me make the dough or fry the tamiya (Sudanese falafels), the same way I used to help in the kitchen back home. Making cultural food is part of our traditions and making Sudanese food is more important for me now, as I want my children to know how to make our food and how to share what we have."
– Sana Elgoraish

Photo: @JonCraig_Photos

SOMALI CRISPY FRIED BLACK-EYED BEAN BHAJIYA

In tribute to Hanna, her close friend Amina has given us a recipe which she knew Hanna loved to eat. Bhajiya is a black-eyed bean fritter or falafel, normally eaten at Ramadan with sambusas and other snacks. Serve hot from the pan with a chilli dipping sauce.

Preparation time: 24 hours • Cooking time: 45 minutes • Makes up to 40

500g black-eyed beans • 1 onion, roughly chopped • 5 cloves of garlic, peeled • Small bunch of fresh coriander, roughly chopped • 1 tsp salt (or more to taste) • ½ tsp baking powder • Oil, for deep frying

Soak the beans in water for 24 hours, then drain them and place in a large blender. Add the onion, garlic, coriander and salt. Blend to a medium paste, not too smooth.

Stir in the baking powder and then form the mixture into spheres the size of ping pong balls. Place them in the fridge while you heat up the oil in a deep pan.

When the oil is hot, gently fry a few of the balls at a time until they are golden brown. Drain on kitchen paper and serve hot with a chilli dipping sauce.

Hanna would say to me: "When people see women like us in the street, they think they know us from our dress and our language, but they don't see who we are." It's hard to capture the essence of a proud Somali woman like Hanna: bright, resilient, resourceful and a doer, dedicated to showcasing her culture and heritage to everyone and using this as a way of building understanding between communities.

She became a familiar face across Bristol, working everywhere to make a difference for others and setting up events to celebrate all the great things from her community. Hanna's trademark smile, her cheekiness and her warmth could move mountains and melt hearts. Her family and friends were her life. Dignified, fun-loving and elegant: there was something in Hanna that we all aspired to be.

When I first met Hanna, I was enthralled by her passion for her heritage. I asked her and her friends to put on an all-woman supper club for 91 Ways, showcasing their culture through their food and showing our city what Somali women really are. The supper club was a great celebration with moving stories, delicious food and Somali drumming and singing. It was an unforgettable evening. Hanna always said that she loved 91 Ways, always appeared at our events and brought laughter.

Sadly, our Hanna passed away in 2020. She was very much part of our 91 Ways community and I am proud to call her Sister. Thank you for sharing your Somali culture, values and your heart with us.

RACHIDA BENSALIMAN

RACHIDA'S MOROCCAN EMPANADAS

Preparation time: 30 minutes • Cooking time: 25 minutes • Makes 10-12

For the dough • 200g flour • 10g sugar • 6g dry active yeast • 5g baking powder • 1 tbsp milk powder • 1 large tbsp butter • 1 tbsp olive oil • 1 tsp vinegar • 1 tsp salt • 1 egg

For the fillings • 3 tbsp olive oil • 2 large onions, finely chopped • 3 cloves of garlic, finely chopped • 200g jarred roasted red peppers, diced • Salt and black pepper • 2 small tins of tuna, drained or 100g baby spinach leaves • 125g feta or soft cheese • 1 egg yolk • 1 tsp semolina • Sesame or onion seeds (optional)

For the dough

Combine all the ingredients in a bowl, then gradually add warm water to bring the dough together. Use as much water as the flour can absorb, then leave the dough to rest for about 10 minutes.

For the filling

Heat the olive oil in a pan, then cook the onion and garlic until soft. Add the roasted red pepper, season with salt and pepper to taste, then cook for about 5 minutes on a low heat. Stir in the tuna.

For a vegetarian version, wash and dry then finely chop the spinach leaves. Cook them with the onion and garlic, then leave the mixture to cool before crumbling in the feta or soft cheese.

To assemble the empanadas

Roll small balls of the dough into thin squares on a lightly floured surface. For best results, roll the pastry firmly away from you two or three times, then give the dough a quarter turn. Dust with flour again if necessary and continue rolling out, frequently turning the pastry so it is not always rolled in the same direction as this causes shrinkage. Use the rolling pin to move the pastry once it's thinner.

Put 1 heaped tablespoon of your filling on one half of each square. Keep the other side clear and fold this over the filling. Seal by pressing the edges with your fingers. You can make the empanadas any shape you like here. Place them all on a lightly greased baking tray.

Mix the egg yolk with the semolina and brush this over the tops of the empanadas. Sprinkle with sesame or onion seeds if using, then I like to cut designs in the pastry. Bake in the oven at 200°c for 18 to 25 minutes until golden brown. Eat with a salad.

Food travels with us; there are so many examples of this. Wherever we go, we find something that feels familiar but is perhaps a different shape, or has different flavours added. The empanada is one of these.

We met Rachida through our 91 Ways ambassador, Negat Hussein. Rachida's life has been very interesting. Moving from Morocco to Spain as a child and then to the UK, she has brought her food inspirations with her and started cooking in the community. She loves cooking and her Instagram account is full of pictures of the fusion of Moroccan and Spanish foods. Of course, Morocco and Spain have an ancient history from the time when Moors occupied many parts of Spain. You can see the mutual influences in the architecture, language, art, music, textiles and of course, the food.

Rachida cooked a Moroccan supper club for us with sumptuous tagines and surprising salads, and taught us how to make Moroccan mint tea: "Always pour from a height into the cup so that the tea bubbles, that is the sign of a good tea!"

These empanadas are Rachida's favourite snack and remind her of the street food life of Morocco.

PURI ALOO

Puri aloo is the quintessential Punjabi comfort food, one that everyone turns to when they need a hug in a bowl: soft, hot and slightly spicy cumin-flecked golden potatoes, eaten with pillowy puffed puri. It was ever present at weekends, lunches and picnics. When I was a child, every bank holiday we would go on a day trip somewhere in England. I think back with warmth at the memories of my father pulling the car over and parking in a quiet country lane, then we would decamp to the grass and my mother would dish out the aloo from a wide brimmed thermos. I can picture it now...and my mouth is watering!

Preparation time: 15 minutes, plus 30 minutes resting • Cooking time: 30 minutes • Serves 4

For the aloo • 4-5 medium potatoes • 2-3 tbsp ghee or neutral oil • ½ tsp cumin seeds • ½ tsp mustard seeds • Pinch of hing (asafoetida) • ½ tsp ground turmeric • ¼ tsp red chilli flakes • Salt, to taste (approx. ½ tsp) • 1 tomato, diced • 1 cup (250ml) boiling water • ½ tsp lemon juice

For the puri • 200g atta (chapati flour) • 50g fine semolina • ½ tsp salt • Neutral oil, for frying

To serve • Fresh coriander leaves • 2 fresh green chillies (optional)

For the aloo

Boil the potatoes in their skins for 15 minutes or until tender, then peel and cut into 2cm cubes. Heat the ghee or oil in a pan, add the cumin and mustard seeds and cook until lightly browned. Stir in the hing, turmeric, chilli flakes and salt. Add the diced potato and tomato, coat them in the spice mixture, then add the boiling water. Cook for about 10 minutes, mashing a few pieces of potato into the gravy to thicken it. Add the lemon juice and adjust the seasoning if needed.

For the puri

Sift all the dry ingredients into a bowl, then start adding water and slowly bring the dough together. Knead and leave to rest for 30 minutes. Knead again for a few minutes and then divide the dough into golf ball sized pieces. Grease a rolling pin and board, then roll each ball thinly into small rounds. Heat the oil in a deep, wide pan. Test the temperature by adding a small piece of dough; if it floats the oil is ready. Fry the rounds of dough in medium to hot oil until golden brown. They should puff up to become light and airy. Drain the fried puri on kitchen roll while you cook the rest.

To serve

Garnish the aloo with the fresh coriander leaves and sliced green chillies, if using. Serve with the puri. They are also good with sabzi, sliced onions and mango pickle.

PUSHPA AUNTY'S BEETROOT CHUTNEY

When I was a teenager, we spent a Christmas with family and friends up north. As was usual in Indian families, the Christmas meal had either Indian additions or spiced up versions of the traditional English dishes. That year, my Pushpa aunty served this beetroot chutney with the turkey and trimmings. It was a flavour sensation, so simple but fresh tasting, cutting through the richness of the other food. I have been making it for around 35 years now and not just for Christmas; it's fantastic with goat's cheese and cold meats too.

Preparation time: 5 minutes • Makes a small bowl

I packet of cooked (not pickled) beetroot • I small onion (red or white) • I fresh green chilli • I lemon, juiced • ½ tsp salt • ½ tsp freshly ground pepper

Finely dice the beetroot, onion and chilli. This can be done by hand but for convenience I do this in the food processor. Put the onion and chilli in first, then add the beetroot and pulse briefly; you do not want a purée. Stir in the lemon juice, salt and pepper before serving.

ROASTED PEANUT CHUTNEY

Preparation time: 5 minutes • Cooking time: 5 minutes • Makes a small bowl

230g unsalted peanuts • Chilli flakes, to taste (I like ¼ tsp) • I medium white onion • Salt, to taste

Roast the peanuts in a hot dry frying pan; don't leave this unattended as they burn quickly. If the peanuts have red skins, you need to remove these after roasting. Put the roasted peanuts and chilli flakes into a powerful blender, quarter and add the onion, then start by adding a tablespoon of water and blend the ingredients together. You are looking for a hummus-like consistency so keep adding water a tablespoon at a time if needed. Add salt to taste before serving.

VIVIANE BOWELL

BOREKAS (MINI CHEESE PIES)

These little pies are special as they remind me of my late sister Claudine. I visited her in West Yorkshire as often as I could when she fell ill. Towards the end she could eat very little, but she still loved these borekas and always asked me to bring some.

Preparation time: 1 hour 15 minutes • Cooking time: 30 minutes • Makes about 25

125ml sunflower oil • 125ml unsalted butter • 125ml water • ½ tsp salt • 550g plain flour • 450g grated cheese (any mixture such as feta, cheddar, gruyere and Emmental) • 1 egg, lightly beaten • 1 egg yolk • Sesame seeds (optional)

Heat the oil and butter in a pan over a low heat until the butter melts. Add the water and salt, mix well, then add the flour gradually. Start with around 250g and mix in with a fork first, then start working it with your hand. Continue adding flour until you have a soft dough that holds together in a ball. Stop mixing as soon as the dough holds together. Cover with cling film and leave it to rest at room temperature for about 20 minutes. Do not put the dough in the fridge.

To make the filling, simply combine the grated cheese with the beaten egg. It should hold together, so if the mixture is runny, add some more grated cheese.

Take walnut-sized lumps of the rested dough and roll each piece into a ball. Press and squash between your palms until you have a 10cm round. Place a heaped teaspoon of the cheese filling into the centre of each round. Fold the dough over the filling into a half-moon, the traditional shape for borekas, then pinch the edges firmly together to seal the pies. Pinch, fold and twist the dough all around the edges or use a fork to seal them. You should be able to make about 25 pies in total.

Place the pies on an oiled tray a few centimetres apart. Beat the egg yolk with a few drops of water and brush this over the pastry. Sprinkle the borekas with sesame seeds if using, then bake at 180°c (160°c fan) for about 30 minutes until slightly golden.

Sana first cooked tamiya (Sudanese falafel) for us at our 91 Ways First International Peace Café. She said that Sudanese falafel are the best in the world and she was right! They were light, spicy, crispy and tasted absolutely delicious.

"The first recipe I'm sharing is for Sudanese tamiya (falafel) which is made in different countries around the world. I like to eat it because it reminds me of my school days in Sudan; it was served in the school canteen but tasted better cooked by the ladies outside the school gates. Nowadays I eat it for breakfast or lunch, occasionally in a sandwich between meals. Back then, I would eat it fresh three or four times a week, as tamiya is one of the main breakfast or late dishes at every event in Sudan: family gatherings, celebrations and very commonly at weddings.

I learnt to make tamiya from my mother and aunts. When I moved to England, I started making it at the weekend with my own family as that was the only day of the week we were at home at the same time and could sit down and share meals. My children help me make the dough or fry the tamiya, the same way I used to help in the kitchen back home. If I have leftover falafel dough which isn't used over the weekend, I make more for work over the following days and share them with my colleagues for lunch. Even when we go to big gatherings in Bristol and need to bring a plate of food, I prefer to make these.

Falafel is a symbolic food in Sudan, which is always eaten the same day it is made, either together as a family or shared with neighbours. Making cultural food is part of our traditions and making Sudanese food is more important for me now, as I want my children to know how to make our food and how to share what we have; it's part of who we are as Sudanese people."

SUDANESE TAMIYA (THE BEST FALAFEL IN THE WORLD)

Preparation time: 20 minutes, plus overnight soaking • Cooking time: 30 minutes • Makes 40-42

500g dried chickpeas • 1 onion, roughly chopped • 4-5 cloves of garlic, peeled • Large handful of fresh dill • 1 tbsp ground cumin • 1 tsp salt • ½ tsp ground coriander • Sprinkle of red chilli powder • 2-3 tbsp breadcrumbs (optional) • 1 egg (optional) • 1 tsp baking powder • At least 2 cups oil (approx. 460g), for frying

Soak the dried chickpeas in water overnight, then drain and rinse them. Combine all the ingredients except the baking powder and oil in a food processor until the mixture is smooth, using the egg and breadcrumbs to bind the dough if needed. Divide the dough in half and keep one half in the fridge for another time. Add the baking powder to the remaining dough (if making the whole batch of falafel at once, double the quantity of baking powder to 2 teaspoons) and mix well.

Heat the oil in a deep frying pan. The oil has to be hot so that the falafel balls dive to the bottom and rise back up again as they cook. The idea is to get them crunchy on the outside but not greasy on the inside. Scoop up a portion of the falafel mix, roll it into a ball between your palms, then flatten slightly by patting the top. Drop it carefully into the hot oil and fry until light brown. Repeat with the remaining mixture, cooking in batches so the pan doesn't get too crowded and the oil stays hot.

Serve the falafel hot for maximum flavour. Tamiya is usually served with other side dishes such as feta cheese, fava beans, aubergine salad and fresh bread.

"Those were the days of miracle and wonder…" as the song goes: the happy days of our childhood. Over-full house crammed with children, parents, grandparents, friends and neighbours, always with open doors! How did we all fit into that small, terraced house? Kitchen activity on high alert – cook, eat, cook, eat – and always standing by to look after everyone. As soon as the doorbell rang, a large pan of hot water would go on the gas to make a milky, spicy, sweet chai and a plate of welcome-to-our-home snacks would appear. No one could leave without eating something. Exhortations to eat filled the air: "eat something, eat more, have another" were the jingles to our childhood.

While weekends were filled with a happy chaos, weekdays were regimented with school and work, except for one evening when we helped Mum fry up the snacks for the weekend to feed any expected or unexpected guests. Our favourite was simple but moreish namak paras, flaky deep-fried flour and cumin strips. Salty and crispy, perfect on the side of a saucer along with cup of sweet tea. We would make mounds of these and fill up huge airtight tubs, set aside for our guests. They were hard to resist though and during the week, hungry from school, we would pull handfuls out and eat them fast before our mum scolded us!

Food, sharing, laughter, friendships, open hearts and sometimes joyful Bollywood dance moves… those really were the days of miracle and wonder!

OUR 'WELCOME' CRISPY NAMAK PARA

This recipe makes thin strips but you can also use the same dough to make mathis, which are a round (but slightly thicker) version and just as delicious. Make loads of these in one go as they will keep for a whole month in an airtight container.

Preparation time: 1 hour • Cooking time: 15-20 minutes
• Serves 8

300g plain flour • 1 tsp salt • ½ tsp carom seeds (ajwain) • ¼ tsp cumin seeds • 2½ tbsp ghee, softened • 150ml warm water (approx.) • Oil, for deep frying

Sift the flour into a large bowl and mix in the salt and seeds with a spoon. Using your hands, combine the dry ingredients with the ghee, crumbling the mixture between your fingers until it has the texture of sand. This takes about 4 or 5 minutes. You can then slowly start adding the warm water. Once the dough has a firm consistency, set it aside for 30 minutes covered with a kitchen towel.

After 30 minutes, divide the dough into small equal-sized balls. Roll out each one into a thin circle. You can now make diamond shapes or straight shapes. For diamond shapes, cut 2cm lengths diagonally across the circle and then do the same again in the opposite direction. Cut the shapes out and place on a greased plate. Repeat with all of the dough.

Heat the oil and test the temperature by dropping in a small bit of dough; the oil should be medium hot to make the namak para crispy and is ready when the dough rises quickly to the top. Gently put in a few pieces at a time and fry until light brown. They will cook quickly, in 1 or 2 minutes. Take out and drain on a piece of kitchen towel. Leave them to cool completely before storing.

MY COOLING RAMADAN ALOO CHAAT

Preparation time: 15 minutes • Cooking time: 15 minutes • Serves 4

4 medium potatoes, peeled • 2 tins of chickpeas • 1 tub of natural yoghurt • 1 tsp ground cumin • 1 tsp red chilli powder (or less, to taste) • 1 tsp garam masala • 1 tsp chaat masala (you can buy this from all supermarkets) • Salt, to taste • 1 small red onion • 2 large fresh tomatoes • 3 tbsp tamarind sauce • 2 fresh green chillies, finely diced (you can use less) • Small handful of fresh coriander leaves, roughly chopped

Cut the potatoes into small cubes and cook in boiling water until soft. Drain and leave to cool. Drain and rinse the chickpeas, then place them in a bowl with the cooled potatoes.

Pour the yoghurt into a large bowl, mix in all the spices and salt, then set aside in the fridge to keep cool. Finely chop the red onion, dice the tomatoes and add both to the bowl of chickpeas and potatoes. Mix gently to combine.

Pour the spiced yoghurt over the potato and chickpea mixture. Drizzle the tamarind sauce over the top. Garnish with the fresh green chillies and coriander. I like to chill this again in the fridge and eat it cold, but it can be eaten at room temperature.

My recipe is for a dish called aloo chaat which we make during Ramadan. Ramadan often falls in the summer months and after a hot day of fasting (no food and no water), we like to break our fast with something cooling, tasty and healthy. Aloo chaat does the trick and is also gentle on the stomach as the yoghurt is healthy and soothing. The Ramadan table is set with snacks such as aloo chaat, samosas and pakoras which we tuck into before our meal. Everyone in my family enjoys these and they are good to share around the table. I still make aloo chaat for my family and children.

Aloo chaat is also a popular street food, both in India and Pakistan: a cooling snack to grab on the way home or out with friends and family. This is my Pakistani version as this is where my family are from. It can be enjoyed as a light salad. In India, the potatoes are often shallow fried first and then added to the chaat.

HANNAH BOATFIELD

Growing up, every holiday was spent at my grandparents' house near the New Forest. To me and my siblings their home brought the biggest contentment imaginable. They ran the village post office and shop, which was attached to their house, and my Grandma Ryle baked fresh cakes and pastries for it every day. We would wake to the smells of these drifting up the stairs, and I would then sit for hours watching her bake, proudly stepping in to 'doink' the sausage rolls when the time came and jostling to be first in line to lick the bowl when the cakes had gone in the oven.

Just the thought of Ryle's cooking brings me comfort. I'd watch her prepare meal after meal while she told me stories that made us both laugh until we cried. Our favourite trip out was to the river that ran through a nearby village, for which she would pack a huge picnic, complete with banana and crisp sandwiches and boiled eggs with a tiny foil wrap of salt to dip them in. We'd often go off foraging among the hedgerows, I would get distracted trying to find four leaf clovers, or eating more blackberries than I took home, and in the summer we'd collect huge heads of elderflower to make this delicious cordial recipe, which was carefully written up in her 'Dodo Book' where all her best recipes were kept.

RYLE'S ELDERFLOWER CORDIAL

My grandma's original recipe used 30g of citric acid as a stabiliser, but you can make this without citric acid as long as you keep it in the fridge and drink within a few weeks, as per this recipe.

Preparation time: However long or short you'd like your foraging walk to be, plus 24 hours • Makes approximately 2.5 litres

12 elderflower heads in full flower, picked with the sun on them • 900g granulated sugar • 2 lemons, sliced • 2.25 litres (4 pints) boiling water

Place the flower heads in a large bowl with the sugar and sliced lemons. Pour over the boiling water and stir well.

Leave the mixture to stand for 24 hours, then strain the cordial through muslin into sterilised bottles. Keep in the fridge for up to a month.

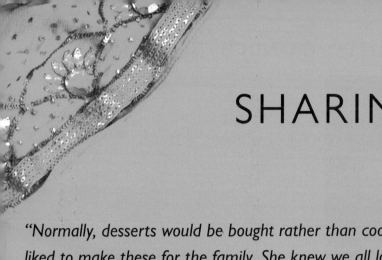

SHARING OUR ... SWEETS

"Normally, desserts would be bought rather than cooked at home, but our grandma liked to make these for the family. She knew we all loved sweet things! One dessert, which was very special, was her sooji halwa… When she made this, we knew she was sharing her love for each one of us." – Shanta Dutta's Grandchildren

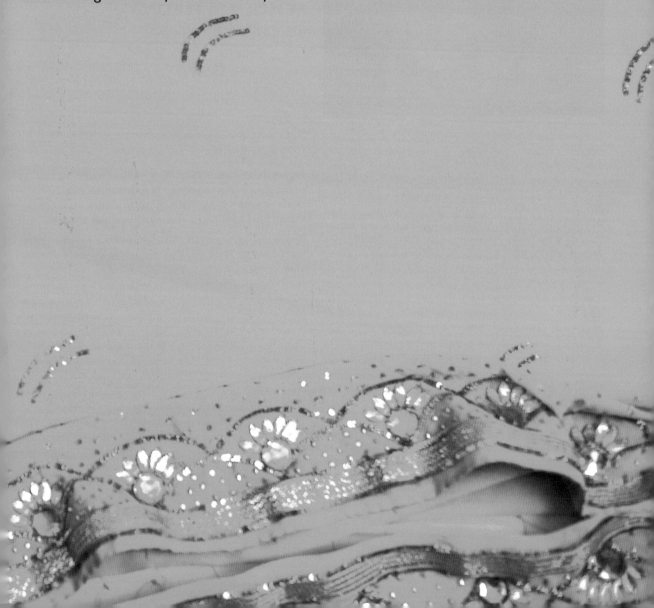

OUR GRANDMOTHER'S SEMOLINA HALWA
(DAADI KA HALWA)

This is a favourite of her son Ravi's and her daughter-in-law, Promila continues to make it. We are so happy that our Nani and Daadi's recipe will live on for future generations of our family.

Preparation time: 15 minutes • Cooking time: 30 minutes • Serves 4

30g whole almonds • 200g sugar • 650ml water • 150g ghee • 150g semolina • 5-6 cardamom pods, smashed open • 25g green sultanas or raisins • Small handful of sliced almonds, pistachios or both

Put the almonds in a bowl, cover them with hot water and leave for 10 minutes. After this time, peel off the skins and slice the almonds.

Make the chasni (sugar syrup) by heating the sugar and water together gently until the sugar dissolves, which will take around 5 to 6 minutes, then take off the heat.

In another pan (we use a heavy karahi or wok), heat the ghee on a low heat and when hot, mix in the semolina and cardamom pods. Keep stirring on a low heat until the mixture becomes a light brown. This should take around 5 or 6 minutes.

Make sure the heat is as low as possible and then start to slowly pour the sugar syrup into the semolina, mixing all the time. The mixture will bubble and may spit, so be careful. Gradually add all the syrup and keep stirring until the halwa leaves the side of the pan and you can see the ghee separating slightly. The halwa should be silky and smooth, not sticky, and cooked well.

Mix in the sultanas or raisins while it's still hot, then discard the cardamom pods. Garnish with the sliced almonds and pistachios, then serve warm.

There are two words for Grandma in Hindi: daadi (meaning paternal grandmother) and nani (meaning maternal grandmother). So, depending on our relationships, we called our grandmother daadi or nani. Shanta Dutta passed away in 2020 when she was 91 years old. She was a force to be reckoned with, the leader of our gang, a great character and a great cook. She cooked calmly and gently with a natural flair and instinct. She worked at BOAC (before it became BA) in their kitchens, where she honed her natural talent and her interest in cooking increased. She learned from chefs who came from all over the world. The work was gruelling as it meant standing for long hours from 6am to 6pm. In the welcome break times (which were short), all the Indian women would sit and share their food and proudly share their recipes. She loved to hear about these recipes and would come home and try them out on us.

Normally, desserts would be bought rather than cooked at home, but our grandma liked to make these for the family. She knew we all loved sweet things! One dessert, which was very special, was her sooji halwa. It's a very sweet, silky smooth and indulgent traditional Hindu and Punjabi dessert. It is also given at the end of Hindu prayers and ceremonies as an offering blessed by God, so we feel blessed when we eat this. When she made this halwa, we knew she was sharing her love for each one of us. Halwa takes time and patience. We often think about her making this in her small kitchen in Southall, stirring the semolina patiently. She would say that the key to the halwa is that it should be 'biscuit' coloured and not darker than this.

DINO'S BOSNIAN BRESKVICE

I met Dino through a friend and the first thing we talked about was food! Dino is a wonderful cook and he is also passionate about his Bosnian heritage. I didn't know anything about Bosnian or Balkan food or the history of this country, apart from a few more recent events which always seemed far away, brutal and confusing.

I was so proud when he and his mum Stela agreed to do a supper club for us so that they could share the story of their heritage through their food. The dishes were so interesting and surprising, illustrating the rich cultural history of the Balkans. They started with a meze, accompanied by a unique, unctuously soft 'butter bread' and followed by a lovely chicken dish, before ending on a Bosnian baklava which even our baklava aficionados said was the best they had ever eaten!

When Dino then spoke about his country, the guests were enthralled. He explained to us that the history of his country, where neighbours and former friends rose up against each other, had taught him that we need to build bridges and to foster mutual understanding to make sure the brutality they faced couldn't be repeated elsewhere. That's why he was so keen to support the efforts of 91 Ways to bring disparate language communities together through food. His wise and heartfelt words will always stay with me. He shares his own recipe and story here. – Kalpna Woolf

"Zdenka Lesko, my maternal grandmother's close friend, lived in a house on a hill a short walk away from our home in Mostar, Bosnia and Herzegovina. As a child I always loved going to Zdenka's. With true Balkan hospitality, Zdenka would go out of her way to make us comfortable on our typically unannounced visits. This always included local style coffee in tiny cups for her and grandmother, as well as plenty of food which often saw fresh vegetables being picked from the garden just for us.

Zdenka was particularly famous for her cakes, including breskvice which means 'little peaches'. These diminutive treats – which really do look like peaches – are stuffed with a rich filling of walnuts and jam. Popular across the former Yugoslavia, especially in winter and for special occasions, they are my childhood favourite dessert. After my mother and I moved to England in 1999, I would always beg my grandmother to bring me little peaches. She would ask Zdenka to make them, and my eyes would light up like beacons every time I saw a tubful coming out of the suitcase. Nobody seemed to make them better than Zdenka.

Years later, when I grew up, I sent my grandmother to ask Zdenka for her recipe and to find out why her little peaches are so delicious. "All recipes are the same, you just have to dedicate yourself to making cakes," was her reply after she gave us her recipe. One week later, in May 2010, Zdenka died from cancer. Today, I make her little peaches for others just like she once made them for me."

BOSNIAN BRESKVICE – LITTLE PEACH CAKES

These are the quantities provided in the original recipe. However, this makes quite a lot. If you're making these for just your own family as opposed to a party, I suggest you scale down to 3 eggs (or even 2) and adjust the rest of the ingredients accordingly.

Preparation time: 1 hour 15 minutes • Cooking time: 20 minutes • Makes enough for a party!

For the dough • **5 eggs** • **100g sugar** • **500g plain flour** • **250ml cooking oil** • **2 tsp baking powder**

For the filling • **150ml good quality jam (cherry works particularly well)** • **100g ground walnuts (optional, though I always put them in)** • **1 tbsp rum (optional)**

To finish • **Red and yellow natural food colouring** • **Sugar**

For the dough

Beat the eggs with the sugar, then add 100g of the flour along with the oil and baking powder. Mix thoroughly, stirring in one direction. Leave to stand for 2 hours. Add the remaining flour gradually and in small batches, stirring in the same direction every time. Keep going until you end up with a smooth, soft dough that is not sticky to the touch, adding a little more flour if needed.

Cut the dough into quarters and, working on a lightly floured surface, roll it into long sausage shapes about 2.5cm thick. Cut these into equal 1.5cm pieces with a sharp knife.

Lightly oil a baking tray or cover with baking paper. One at a time, roll the dough pieces between the palms of your hands into even, smooth balls. There must not be any cracks, and the balls must be as perfectly spherical as possible. Place them on the baking tray with a 2cm gap between each.

Preheat the oven to 160°c (140°c fan) and then bake the dough balls for about 20 minutes or until just starting to turn brown. Remove and leave to cool completely.

On the flat side of the dough balls, carefully make a series of cuts all around the edge and gently push inwards to make an indentation. Scrape out more of the indentation to enlarge it, reserving all the cake crumbs in a bowl. Be careful not to go all the way through or use too much force so the dough balls don't fall apart.

For the filling

Combine the reserved cake crumbs with the jam, ground walnuts and rum (if using). Taste the mixture and adjust the amounts as required, adding some sugar if it's not sweet enough. Using a teaspoon, fill two of the hollowed-out dough balls with the jam mixture. Carefully press them together and you have one completed breskvica! Repeat with all the other dough balls.

To finish

In two small bowls, dissolve each food colouring in a little water. Fill another bowl with plenty of sugar. One by one and working quickly, dip each complete breskvica into the food colouring so they end up half yellow and half red. Roll the wet breskvica in the sugar, making sure the entire surface is coated. Repeat with all the other breskvice until you have a pile of 'little peaches' to enjoy.

Tamina is an Algerian dessert of coarse semolina steeped in fragrant orange blossom and honey. Eaten by new mothers, it's both served to and gifted by streams of guests for up to a month. It's also eaten to celebrate the prophet Muhammad's birthday, Mouloud. The main ingredients represent sustenance (semolina), love (honey) and the rich blessings of Allah (butter).

News reaches my aunt's kitchen of a neighbour's newborn and we gather to prepare tamina. We toast semolina in a hot pan until it turns from yellow to golden brown. Across North Africa, semolina is eaten for breakfast, lunch and dinner, and is traditionally hand rolled into couscous. In the hot month of August my aunts will spend a week making enough couscous to see them through the winter months. Sitting on the ground with large aluminium bowls between their legs, they rub the semolina between their palms, lifting it above their heads and letting it fall back into the bowl. They flick water and oil over the mixture to bind it, and then shake it through a tambourine-shaped sieve, separating the couscous balls from the semolina. This is repeated up to four times until every grain has formed fluffy couscous balls and is then laid out to dry in the heat of the sun.

We melt the butter and stir in the honey, lifting the mixture and watching it drip from the spoon. Today we've bought butter from the local town, a luxury for my grandmother who made it for most of her life. We mix together the semolina, butter and honey to form a thick paste. Orange blossom is sprinkled over the mixture, filling the kitchen with the smell of summer. We remember sugary coffees served with orange flowers plucked from the trees and chewy orange jam.

We pat the mixture into a shallow glass bowl and spoon over a layer of honey. Everyone has their own decoration of cinnamon, Turkish delight, and almonds. In my family we wet the bottom of a glass and dust it with cinnamon to print a series of overlapping circles. We sprinkle the cinnamon into the shape of a Y in the centre, representing the newborn's name, Younes. The new mother joins us around a table and the tamina is plated up onto saucers and served with teaspoons.

ALGERIAN TAMINA
(TOASTED SEMOLINA WITH ORANGE BLOSSOM)

Preparation time: 5 minutes • Cooking time: 45 minutes
• Serves 4-6

175g semolina (coarse or medium) • 3 tbsp unsalted butter • 2 tbsp honey, plus extra for serving • 2 tbsp orange blossom water • Ground cinnamon, for decoration

In a hot pan, toast the semolina, stirring it continuously to avoid it burning on the bottom. When the mixture has turned a nutty brown colour, take it off the heat and set aside.

In a separate pan, melt the butter and then stir in the honey. Mix the toasted semolina into the honey and butter mixture until you have a thick paste.

Stir in the orange blossom, then taste it and see if you'd like to add more. Pat the tamina into a serving bowl, and spoon over a thin layer of honey.

Wet the bottom of a circular object, dip it into the ground cinnamon, and then create a series of overlapping circles on top of the tamina for decoration. Serve in small portions.

BSL is one of the 91 languages spoken in Bristol. I was so delighted that Yvonne, who loves food, agreed to share her story and a handwritten recipe from her mum with us.

"My name is Yvonne, also known as the Deaf Nigella, and I am a bubbly businesswoman, food and lifestyle vlogger as well as an amazing cook; I am known among my friends as the queen of soup and salads! In my other side job, I am a TV presenter for the BBC's See Hear and have presented TV cooking segments in sign language.

I was born Deaf, and in fact there are three generations of Deaf people in my family. It was my mum, Davina Momber, who really inspired my love of food and cooking. It was fantastic growing up with a Deaf mum who was a first-class cook and hostess; we always had a house full of people and mealtimes were always the times that we felt most connected. I was inspired by my mother to be able to carry on these traditions with my own family. I am married with three children, and we love to cook together and welcome guests as a family.

In 2016 I decided to set up my own catering business, Yumma Food, which seeks to educate the Deaf community about the importance of nutrition and the impact that food has on our wellbeing and general health. I have a very holistic attitude towards wellbeing and the importance of using food to promote wellness. Sadly, some Deaf people haven't previously had opportunities to learn about nutrition, so I have been busy creating vlogs, in both British Sign Language and English, to share some of this knowledge.

I am really proud of what I have managed to achieve with Yumma Food. It has definitely boosted my confidence and I have really learned a lot about myself. My passion is for TV cooking, but I would also love to train as a life coach and inspire others to use food in the way that my mother inspired me. My mother is now 89, but still lives independently and is still cooking. She has been a phenomenal role model, not just for me but for the whole of the Deaf community."

MY MUM'S LEMON FLAN

Preparation time: 15 minutes, plus 4 hours setting
• Cooking time: 15 minutes • Serves 4-6

**For the base • 225g digestive biscuits • 115g butter
• 55g sugar**

**For the filling • 4 large lemons • 340ml condensed milk
• 285ml double cream**

Preheat the oven to 180°c. Crush the biscuits. Melt the butter in a pan and then add the sugar. Stir in the biscuit crumbs until well combined. Press the base into a small, greased flan dish, then bake in the preheated oven for 8 minutes. Set aside to cool.

Zest and then juice both the lemons. Whisk the condensed milk until smooth, stir in the lemon zest and then slowly blend in the cream and lemon juice.

Pour the lemon mixture gently into the flan dish over the base and chill for 4 hours, or until set.

AZZA MUSTAFA

I grew up in the Sudan alongside my mum and two sisters, and conversations in my family have always been about food and what we are going to cook for the next meal. I've definitely picked up their love for food along the way.

After I married and had three children, I realised that my mother's food has a flavour and taste not comparable with other food. I just want to bring all my lovely mum's food to my family and to make something to remind me of her. Her baseema is one of my favourite dishes; Mum cooked it every Thursday and the flavour is incredible.

SUDANESE SWEET BASEEMA CAKE

Preparation time: 20 minutes • Cooking time: I hour
• Serves 6-8

For the cake • 60g flour • 250g semolina • 60g coconut flakes • I tsp baking powder • 2 eggs • 125g yoghurt • 125g unsalted butter • A dash of vanilla extract

For the syrup • 125g sugar • 125g water • I tsp lemon juice • A dash of vanilla extract

For the topping • Jam of your choice • Coconut flakes

For the cake
Sieve the flour into a bowl and combine it with the semolina, coconut flakes and baking powder. In a second bowl, whisk the eggs together then add the yoghurt, butter and vanilla. Mix until smooth. Combine the wet ingredients with the dry ingredients until the cake batter is smooth again. Spread it over a tray lined with baking paper, then bake in a preheated oven for 30 minutes at 180°c.

For the syrup
While the cake is cooking, prepare the syrup by combining all the ingredients in a pan and heating them gently until the sugar has completely dissolved and the syrup has slightly thickened.

For the topping
When the cake is ready, pour the syrup over the top before it has cooled. Once it soaks in, spread your choice of jam over the cake and sprinkle with coconut flakes. Allow to cool before serving.

GRANDMA EMILIA'S KITNIKEZ (APPLE CHEESE)

This sweet delight is normally made in the north of Bosnia and Herzegovina, where the Austro-Hungarian influence was much stronger than in the south. One piece is plenty to satisfy a sweet tooth or enjoy with coffee as a pick-me-up. In Spain, it's known as membrillo and is eaten with cheese.

Preparation time: 25 minutes, plus 3-4 weeks setting • Cooking time: 2 hours • Makes about 40 squares

---

3kg apples • 1 litre water • 1.5kg sugar (approx.) • 2 lemons, juiced • Walnut halves

Peel, core and chop the apples. Put them into a large saucepan, add the water and cook for about 30 minutes until mushy (if you can get apples with deep red skin, leave some unpeeled as this will colour your mixture nicely). Drain off all but 100ml of the liquid.

Blend the apple mixture with a stick blender. Weigh this purée and add half of that weight in sugar to the pan (it may be more or less than the 1.5kg stated above). Stir in the lemon juice and cook on a low heat, stirring frequently, for about 1 hour 30 minutes until you have a thick apple paste. The aim is to reduce as much moisture as possible to speed up the drying process.

Lightly oil a rectangular dish (I used a Pyrex) and pour the apple mixture in. Level the surface, then place the walnut halves on top and slightly push them in. Leave the kitnikez to cool completely for 24 hours. After that, keep it in a well-ventilated area and flip the whole set jelly over every 2 to 3 days to expose each side in turn and speed up the drying process.

After 3 to 4 weeks, the kitnikez will be ready. Cut into about 40 squares, depending on the size of your dish, then roll them in sugar and serve. This can keep for a long time (at least 6 months) if it survives that long. Enjoy!

EUNICE'S BUTTERY ECCLES CAKES

If you have time, homemade puff pastry is of course much better than shop-bought. Don't forget that all the butter has to be from New Zealand!

Preparation time: 15 minutes • Cooking time: 15-20 minutes • Makes 12

600g all-butter puff pastry • 40g unsalted butter • 200g currants • 50g mixed peel • 100g light muscovado sugar • 1 tsp ground cinnamon • 1 tsp ground ginger • 1 tsp allspice • 1 orange, zested • 1 free-range egg white • 75g Demerara sugar

My recipe is in honour of a dear family friend, Eunice, who was the mum of a friend to my mum growing up. Eunice and her husband Jeff befriended my grandparents and became firm family friends. Sadly, my grandad suddenly passed away months before I was born, and Eunice and Jeff were a great support and comfort to my family. They became the unofficial third set of grandparents to myself and my brother as we grew up, fuelling our love for travel through their own travel stories and of course through recipe sharing. Eunice would send cuts of recipes she thought we would like, and wrote out by hand her own personal favourites, which all had to use New Zealand butter as, to her, it was the finest you could get.

Eunice's Eccles cakes were buttery and crumbly with caramelised shards of sugar and a fruit filling that packed a spiced punch. On one visit I misheard her offering them, and thought they were called Ethel's cakes, which brought tears of laughter to Eunice's twinkling eyes. From then on, they were known as Ethel's cakes in our family.

I have collected all the recipes that Eunice sent to me in a book and it is one of my most treasured possessions. Sadly, she passed away a few years ago at a very ripe old age, but I often see recipes or postcards that make me think of her and it brings such warmth to me. I make these Ethel's cakes on occasions which mean a lot to my family and can't help but think of Eunice when I'm making them, always with a smile.

If you're making your own puff pastry, prepare it now to allow it time to rest before rolling. If using shop-bought, remove ready-rolled pastry from the fridge 30 minutes before starting to make the Eccles cakes, allowing it to soften and become easier to use. Otherwise, roll out the pastry to the thickness of a £1 coin. You should now be able to cut out 12 circles of pastry, each 12cm in diameter.

Preheat the oven to 200°c and line two baking trays with parchment paper. In a large pan, melt the butter and then take it off the heat before stirring in the dried fruit, mixed peel, sugar, spices and orange zest until well mixed.

Dampen the edge of a pastry disc with water, place a good tablespoon of filling in the centre and bring the pastry together to enclose the filling, pinching the edges to seal it in. Turn the Eccles cake over so the join is underneath and place on the prepared tray. Flatten gently until the ball is an oval shape and the fruit starts to poke through the top. Repeat with the remaining pastry discs and filling.

Cut two little slits in the top of each cake, then brush them with the egg white and liberally sprinkle with the Demerara sugar.

Bake the Eccles cakes in the preheated oven for 15 to 20 minutes until they are a deep golden colour. Leave to cool for 10 minutes to let the sugar settle. You don't have to let them cool completely before eating though; they are best when still warm. Eccles cake can also be served with sharp crumbly cheese, preferably a Lancashire wedge.

OLA'S MAZUREK

I am forever grateful for the joy of growing up in a very close and loving family in Poland. I have been so lucky to have had my sister, my parents and both sets of grandparents all around me throughout my childhood. This is the main reason I have always loved holidays and festivities – exciting times with activities and traditions that we all shared in – and of course food was a huge part of that.

In my hometown – historic Sandomierz in the south of Poland – my Babcias (grandmothers) lived at opposite ends of the park, and it was easy to visit them both. I loved spending days in their gardens, picking fresh fruit and flowers. At Christmas, we made mountains of sticky dumplings with wild mushrooms and delicious crimson beetroot soup. We always decorated the house and dressed the Christmas tree together. On Wigilia (Christmas Eve) I had to restrain myself, as there were two feasts to attend – one with each Babcia – which meant more food and more presents!

Easter was always my favourite celebration as there was even more to do together. Firstly, paint the eggs and prepare a small food basket to take to the church to be blessed. Secondly, so many cakes to bake! Not only to eat but also as part of our Easter display. This is the tradition that I associate with my Babcia Dana, who is turning 95 as I write this! We used to make a babka (a dome-shaped pound cake) together each year, and many variations of mazurek (shortcrust pastry with various toppings). Mazurek was the most exciting to me because as well as the grown-up versions, I always had my own smaller square or egg-shaped bases to decorate however I wanted.

Since moving to England – even if I can't get home to my family – I still always make mazurek and the traditional decorations at Easter. I really enjoy cooking and experimenting and have evolved the original recipes, combining elements of Mum and Grandma's versions with my own and my husband's favourite ingredients. Enjoy!

POLISH EASTER CAKE (MAZUREK)

These are the quantities I use for a 20 by 20cm tin and a few extra small shapes. For larger tins, scale up the ingredients accordingly but do not add more egg white, just additional yolks.

Preparation time: 2 hours • Cooking time: 1 hour • Serves 2

For the toppings • 2 thick-skinned oranges • 250g caster or granulated sugar • 100g milk chocolate, chopped • 100g dark chocolate, chopped • 50g unsalted or lightly salted butter, cubed • Mix of roughly chopped nuts (I use almonds, hazelnuts, walnuts) plus extra for decoration

For the dough • 250g plain flour • 50g caster sugar • ½ tsp baking powder • 50g cold margarine or baking spread (such as Stork) • 1 whole egg • 1 egg yolk

For the toppings

You can make these a few hours or a day ahead. Wash the oranges, put them in a pan and completely cover with cold water. Bring to the boil, then lower the temperature and cook for about 45 minutes or until the oranges are soft. Drain off the water and leave to cool. Slice the oranges into 2-3mm rings on a plate to catch the juice. Don't worry if they fall apart but try to keep the skin in long strings if you can. Put the oranges and juice back into the pan on the heat, add the sugar and 1 to 2 tablespoons of water, then stir gently until sugar dissolves. Simmer for a good 30 minutes, or until the liquid turns into a thick syrup. Transfer to a bowl, cover and set aside at room temperature.

For the dough

Combine the dry ingredients and then grate in the margarine or add in small cubes. Stir in the whole egg and yolk, then mix until you have a crumbly dough. Add a bit more flour or a splash of water if required. Refrigerate for 30 minutes.

Preheat the oven to 160-180°c. Roll out the chilled dough directly on a sheet of baking paper, to fit the dimensions of your tin at about 5-7mm thickness. Transfer the sheet to the tin and use a rolling pin or your fingers to flatten out any remaining bits of dough, then cut out some Easter shapes. Bake the base and extra biscuits in the preheated oven for about 20 to 25 minutes, or until golden.

Meanwhile, put the prepared oranges in a sieve over a bowl and leave them to drain. Keep the syrup. Melt the chopped chocolate and butter in a heatproof bowl over a pan of simmering water. Stir until smooth, then take off the heat and add chopped nuts to taste.

Once the pastry base has cooled down, start adding the toppings. Arrange the oranges into a single layer about 1cm deep in ring shapes or strips. Once the whole base is covered with orange peel, you can drizzle some syrup on top, but not too much, as otherwise the pastry will turn soggy. Cover the oranges with a layer of the nutty chocolate glaze about 5-7mm deep, then decorate with the extra nuts. Decorate the extra pastry shapes and refrigerate any remaining oranges and syrup.

MY NAN'S APPLE PIE
(AND JAM TURNOVER)

Preparation time: 30 minutes • Cooking time: 40 minutes
• Makes a 30cm (12 inch) pie and 1 small turnover

225g butter, diced and chilled • 450g plain flour • Pinch of salt • 1 small egg • 450g cooking apples • 100g sugar • Grated nutmeg, to taste • 1 egg, beaten with a splash of milk • 1 tbsp jam of your choice

There are so many stories about food running through our communities, each with its own history, waiting to be discovered or passed on and then slightly changed for the next generation. It has always been my intention to write about this recipe, as it's one of my earliest food memories. Back then I could barely see over the counter of the kitchen work surface in my Nan's three-bed then council house in Stockwood. I practically grew up there and still visited for dinner more than twice a week way into my working life. Food was always at the centre of her home, and it was a comfort and retreat to enjoy the simple freshly cooked food I grew up with.

I watched this pie being made in the same way over and over, year on year, always using the same enamel tin to bake it in, the same knife to cut the apples. The apples never even touched the board, but were just sliced against the thumb (as were the potatoes for Nan's home-cooked chips). The pastry ingredients were always weighed in heaped tablespoons, but I have used gram measurements here to ensure the recipe works for you too.

Rub the chilled butter into the flour with the tips of your fingers, then add the salt. Beat the egg separately and use two thirds of it to bring the mixture together into a dough. Shape this into a ball and place in the fridge while you deal with the filling. Peel and slice the cooking apples, then toss them with the sugar and grated nutmeg.

Preheat the oven to 170°c. Roll out the chilled pastry to a thickness of about 3mm and use half of it to line an enamel baking tin of about 30cm (12 inches) in diameter. Unless your tin is non-stick, grease and line it before laying on the pastry.

Place the apple filling evenly inside the dish and brush the pastry rim with the beaten egg and milk mixture. Top the pie with the other half of the rolled-out pastry, then press the edges together with a fork all the way round. Trim off the excess, egg wash the top and sprinkle with sugar if you fancy.

Bake the pie in the preheated oven for 40 minutes. Meanwhile, roll the leftover pastry into a 20cm (8 inch) circle and spread the jam in the centre. Egg wash the edges, turn them over to make a parcel and seal with a fork. Place the turnover on a baking tray, brush the pastry with egg wash and sprinkle with sugar if you like. Bake in the hot oven for 20 minutes so the jam turnover is ready at the same time as your apple pie. This was the bit I always looked forward to the most!

BRINDA BUNGAROO
MAURITIAN DHUD PITTI

Preparation time: 30 minutes • Cooking time: 1 hour • Serves 4

For the pasta • 1 cup (approx. 132g) plain flour • Pinch of salt • Cold water • For the dish • 250g dried rice pasta • 1 tbsp ghee, butter or coconut oil • Handful of chopped raisins or currants and almonds • 1 litre whole milk (or a mixture of condensed milk and whole milk) • ½ tin of coconut milk • ½ vanilla pod • ½ tsp ground green cardamom • 2 tbsp desiccated coconut • 100g sugar (depending on how sweet you like it) • Handful of chopped mixed nuts (I used almonds, pistachios, walnuts and hazelnuts) • Handful of chopped pistachios, for garnishing

For the pasta

Place the flour in a mixing bowl, add the salt, make a well and then start adding cold water until you reach a firm dough consistency. Cover and leave to rest for at least 10 minutes. Form the rested dough into little rice shapes by putting little pieces in the palm of your hand and using the heel of the other hand to push and shape them. They can now be cooked fresh or left to dry completely. If storing, spread the pasta shapes out on a floured tray so they do not stick together. Leave to air dry. Just like pasta, once dried they can be stored in a jar and will keep for months. To speed up the cooking process, I advise soaking the dried pasta in cold water for a few hours first.

For the dish

Bring a deep saucepan of water to the boil. Add the dried rice pasta and cook until al dente, then drain and set aside.

Meanwhile, melt the ghee, butter or coconut oil in a heavy-based pan, then add the chopped raisins and almonds. Toss in the hot fat until light brown. Pour the whole milk and coconut milk into the pan and heat gently, taking care it does not overspill. If preferred, you can use the whole tin of coconut milk here.

Split the vanilla pod in half lengthways and scrape out the seeds. Add these to the milk mixture along with the ground cardamom and the drained rice pasta. Slowly bring to the boil, then lower the heat and simmer rapidly, stirring from time to time to prevent the pasta from sticking to the bottom of the pan. If using condensed milk, add it to the mixture now.

Simmer while stirring occasionally until the liquid has reduced by about half. This may take some time but be patient, as the cooking process is slow but worthwhile. Once reduced, taste the mixture to check for sweetness and add sugar if needed. Add the coconut and mixed nuts, stir well, then transfer the dhud pitti into serving bowls. Finish with a sprinkle of chopped pistachios.

Brinda's Note: As this pasta is flour-based, it tends to absorb a lot of liquid, so you may find it dries out when it is cold. To serve from chilled, add a little more milk while you warm it.

Lately I have been trying to replicate some of the traditional and homely dishes my grandmother and mum used to make. One of them is this humble homemade delicacy called dhud pitti, which resembles rice but is made with flour and is actually tiny pasta shapes, similar to orzo, cooked in an aromatic milk with added nuts, raisins and coconut. It's the perfect breakfast or anytime treat.

My grandmother used to make them; she would sit down on a small bench with a large tray in front of her, and one by one patiently shape the dough into tiny rice-shaped pasta pieces. These would then be left to dry until they turned hard. Once dried they would be stored and, like dried pasta, would keep well in an airtight container.

It is true that getting older makes people wiser, or at least I hope so in my case. Since I now appreciate simple staple foods more, that also takes me down memory lane. So, I wish to share this delicious but simple pasta-like dish. My dad really liked this dish, as he especially enjoyed homemade simple dishes and had even more affinity with sweet dishes like this one.

MICHAL NAHMAN

MICHAL'S BAKED CARDAMOM-ROSE KATAIF

Around three years ago I began to cook a weekly vegetarian feast at a sustainable woodland called The Cherrywood Project, near Marshfield. I had gone to the woods that day to learn about sustainability and somehow managed to become the chef instead! After gaining familiarity with the kitchen and the project, I went there once a week for a year and half to feed the workers in an off-grid open fire kitchen. I brought influences from my home: Balkan, Turkish, Middle Eastern and North African flavours are the ones I grew up on.

This trip to the woods was the start of a journey exploring the meanings of home, belonging and not belonging. Eventually I hosted a large five course feast for a charity I'm a trustee of, called Project MAMA (which supports migrant women through pregnancy and birth, www.projectmama.org) and ran a day-long cookery workshop in the woods, teaching people to make their own fires, and to cook the foods of my home.

The more I did this, the more I began to ask what home means, how does one come to 'belong' somewhere and how do some foods get characterized as 'belonging' to a place. Some of the foods I cooked, people recognized as Palestinian, others as Israeli, Turkish, Arabic, Maghrebi. Food travels across regions with people and becomes not only sustenance for the body, but also for larger imaginings of bigger things, like culture, politics and memory. And this has driven me to begin collecting the stories of other Middle Eastern and North African descended Jewish people, or Mizrachi for short. This collection of Bristol-based foodies, who are writing and cooking the food of their families, are generously sharing their stories with me in this newly born project.

After living in the UK for 20 years, I finally feel more at home, immersed as I am in gathering stories from others about the themes I'm exploring in The Mizrachi Food Project. I'm learning so much about the foods of my Turkish and Balkan ancestors: fire roasted peppers and aubergines, slow cooked meat, beans and pulses, sweet and fragrant desserts.

My father's family come from a small village called Bayramiç near the seaside town of Çanakkale, where the battle of Troy took place. On Friday nights they would eat Avicas con Arroz (small white beans in a tomato base, with only a tiny bit of meat and lots of rice – they were humble people, with humble foods). On Saturday mornings the men of my family would each pray in their homes, the Sabbath prayers, and the women would pack a hearty brunch meal. Off they would go to the woods with a rug to sit on. Once there, they would arrange their rugs in a circle and do the Shabbat Kiddush (blessing) together. Most Jews bless the wine but in my Turkish family the blessing was with Arak, the aniseed spirit drunk in many parts of the Arab world. And then they would eat their Shabbat picnic in the woods.

The dish I have shared in this book is a sweet and fragrant dessert that I created, which takes inspiration from different foods such as the Palestinian kanafe (a cheesy filo dessert invented in Nablus in the 10th century) and the tel kataifi (cream-filled) dessert that is found in Turkey, Greece, Israel, the Balkans and the Levant. I brought it together with a seasonal fruit, apricots, and a Turkish clotted cream known as kaimak (also found across the Middle East and Balkans) and mixed it with syrup I had made from pale pink roses that grow in my garden and cracked cardamom pods.

BAKED CARDAMOM-ROSE KATAIF WITH FIRE ROASTED APRICOTS AND KAIMAK

This dessert featured on my menu at both the Cherrywood Feast and cookery course. It makes 10 to 12 servings because you will want more than just one! The noodle-like filo pastry known as kataif can be bought in most Middle Eastern shops, as can the kaimak and rosewater or rose petal jam.

Preparation time: 15 minutes • Cooking time: 20-30 minutes • Makes 10-12

300-500ml water • 250g caster sugar • 2-3 tbsp rosewater or rose petal jam • 6 cardamom pods, cracked • 500g soft fruit, such as apricots • 200-300g unsalted cold butter • 1 pack of kataif (shredded filo) • 400g kaimak (Turkish cream) • Roasted almonds or pistachios, crushed (optional)

Preheat your oven to 160°c fan (180°c). First, make your syrup so it can cool and the flavours infuse while you prepare the rest of the dessert. In a small pan, gently heat the water and sugar until the sugar has dissolved. Add the rosewater or jam (use a bit less sugar if you are using jam) and cardamom pods, then remove the pan from the heat. Set aside to cool.

Meanwhile, prepare your apricots by halving them and taking out the stones. Cut the cold butter into small rectangles, about the size of Lego blocks, and set aside.

On a flat, clean and dry surface, carefully separate out the kataif pastry strands into several small rows or bunches (like separating out long hair when making a thin plait). At the base of each row, on the closest side to you, place a small chunk of cold butter. Then roll the pastry noodles around and upward so they make a tight little roll. Pack the rolls closely into a buttered roasting tin. Bake them for around 20 to 30 minutes, depending on the heat of your oven. They are toasted brown when ready.

When the pastry has about 15 minutes left to cook, begin to grill your fruit. You can do this either in a flat or ridged pan with a few drops of olive oil, or butter. Do grill it on a fire if you have access to one though; the smokiness of the fire makes this a real treat! You want these to be warm but not too hot when you serve the dessert.

As soon as the pastry comes out of the oven, pour the cooled sweet syrup over them. Place them in a bowl, small plate or even a pretty china teacup. Place a grilled apricot onto each plate. Gently place a tablespoon of the kaimak on top of the pastry, then top with roasted and crushed almonds or pistachios if you fancy it.

BETH OSBORNE

I have fond memories of cooking with my grandmother as a child. She had a huge rhubarb patch at the bottom of the garden, and I remember going there with her to harvest what we needed. I loved to pull the pink stalks of rhubarb from the ground and then she would let me use a knife to cut off the huge green leaves. Her kitchen was small but I was fascinated by her larder, which contained paper-covered shelves filled with carefully arranged jars and tins. In pride of place for me was a green glass sugar shaker with a silver top. It was presented on the table along with the rhubarb crumble and we loved using it to shake an extra dusting of sugar onto our crumble, which was always served in an enamelware dish.

GRANDMA HARE'S RHUBARB CRUMBLE

Preparation time: 25 minutes • Cooking time: 30 minutes • Serves 4

500g rhubarb • 100g sugar • I orange, zested and juiced • 85g cold butter, cubed • 175g self-raising flour • 50g sugar

Preheat the oven to 200°c (180°c fan or Gas Mark 6) while you prepare the crumble filling and topping. First, cut the rhubarb into 2.5cm chunks and put them into a saucepan with the 100g of sugar, orange zest and orange juice.

Cook the rhubarb mixture on a low heat, letting it simmer until the rhubarb is soft, then transfer it to a medium-sized ovenproof dish ready for the topping.

Make the topping by rubbing the cold cubes of butter into the flour with your fingertips until the mixture looks like breadcrumbs. Add the 50g of sugar and stir through so it's evenly distributed.

Scatter the topping over the stewed rhubarb and bake the crumble in the preheated oven for 30 minutes until the top is golden brown. Serve with custard, vanilla ice cream or thick cream.

HOLI TREAT MALPURA

Preparation time: 10 minutes, plus 3-40 minutes resting
• Cooking time: 35 minutes • Makes about 10

For the malpura • 135g plain flour • 50g dried milk
powder • 1 tbsp sugar • 1 tsp crushed fennel seeds • ¼ tsp
baking powder • A pinch of salt • 395ml warm milk
• 2 tbsp plain yoghurt, beaten • Ghee or oil, for frying
• Crushed pistachios, to garnish

For the sugar syrup • 200g sugar • 180ml water • A few
strands of saffron • ¼ tsp ground green cardamom • 1 tsp
lemon juice

For the malpura

Mix the flour, milk powder, sugar, fennel seeds, baking powder
and salt together in a large bowl. Stir in the warm milk, beating
the mixture so there are no lumps. Add the beaten yoghurt and
mix well until the batter is a thick pouring consistency, then
leave it to rest for 30 to 40 minutes.

Heat the ghee or oil to a depth of 0.5cm (¼ of an inch) in a frying
pan. Take a small ladleful of batter and pour it into the pan.
Lower the heat and cook the malpura on both sides until golden
brown. Transfer to a plate lined with kitchen paper and repeat
until all the batter is used up.

For the sugar syrup

Mix the sugar, water, saffron and ground cardamom together in
a small pan on a medium heat. Once the sugar has dissolved,
add the lemon juice and simmer the syrup for 4 to 5 minutes.
Remove from the heat and set aside.

To serve

Heat the sugar syrup to a warm temperature. Dip the malpura
in the syrup for 30 seconds, then remove and place on a plate.
Garnish with the crushed pistachios and serve with more plain
yoghurt.

I remember how excited we all used to get near Holi time. Not
only did we get a holiday from school, Mum would make
delicious food for us too. Malpura, a sweet pancake-style
dessert, was my favourite. It was also made for weddings and
my mum used to make it on rainy days with pakoras as well. It's
amazing how we now remember childhood food. Mum never
weighed out any ingredient. It was always a handful of this and a
pinch of that, so here's the recipe but please note that the
measurements are approximate. I hope you like it! Make and
enjoy this special treat without worrying about the calories.

For me, sharing food and recipes means extending a hand of friendship to other fellow beings, an invitation to share in those precious aspects of life: caring for each other, love and laughter. Sharing homemade food is also about giving something created with one's own hands, passing on positive energy. I have selected a couple of recipes that typify Bosnia, the country I come from, a melting pot of civilisations, cultures and traditions. They are rooted in bountiful nature and the history that brought culinary influences from the Byzantine, Roman, Ottoman and Austro-Hungarian empires.

Generations of Bosnian women have transformed simple ingredients that nature provided into morsels of delight that we enjoy today. Among my most treasured possessions is a collection of recipes that my maternal and paternal grandmothers, my auntie and my mum gave me as I was leaving for the United Kingdom. Not only an expression of our culture and identity, evoking the taste of sun-kissed summers and snow-swept winters, they are also a connection to strong women in my family, who knew how to keep their families going through huge historical events affecting their lives. They are a testament to continuity and hope. It is these handwritten recipes that I consulted for this book, selecting two dishes that will nourish your body and soul.

BAYADERA

This elegant yet simple sweet treat is a perfect accompaniment to a cup of coffee and a chat with a friend. It is one of my maternal grandmother's favourite recipes, often part of a larger selection of small fancies. There is no baking involved and it's quite quick to make.

Preparation time: 45 minutes, plus chilling time • Cooking time: 10 minutes • Makes about 30 pieces

100g unsalted butter • 125g digestive biscuits • 125g caster sugar • 1 egg • 125g ground almonds or walnuts • 20g cocoa powder • For the chocolate glaze • 75g dark chocolate (I use 72%) broken up • 15-30g caster sugar • 75ml milk • Splash of water • Small knob of unsalted butter (the size of an almond)

Leave the butter to stand at room temperature until soft while you crush the digestive biscuits into fine crumbs. With a handheld mixer, combine the soft butter with the sugar in a bowl. Add the egg and continue mixing until incorporated, then add the biscuit crumbs and ground nuts. Mix well.

Put half the biscuit mixture into another bowl, add the cocoa powder to the remaining half and mix until fully blended. Grease a 20 by 20cm tin and sprinkle some breadcrumbs or extra biscuit crumbs over the base to make it easier to take the bayaderas out. Spread the cocoa crumb mixture into the prepared tray and place in the fridge for about 10 minutes to firm up slightly.

Once cooled, spread the remaining crumb mixture on top and place in the fridge for another 10 minutes. In the meantime, make the chocolate glaze. Put the chocolate, milk and sugar into a heatproof bowl with a splash of water and melt the mixture over a saucepan of simmering water until the consistency is smooth and even. Leave the glaze to cool off the heat.

Take the tray out of the fridge and pour the chocolate glaze over the top as the final layer. Tilt the tray from side to side until the glaze has evenly covered the entire surface. Leave in the fridge to cool down for a few hours, or even overnight. Keep chilled and when you're ready to serve the bayadera, cut into small rectangles (about 5 by 2cm) and serve with coffee or after dinner.

DAVID HARDMAN (AND HIS DAUGHTER ELIZA MORELAND)

DAVID & ELIZA'S CLOOTIE DUMPLING

My parents, my sister and I lived with my Nana and Grandad Whyte in Aberdeen from 1944 until 1952. My grandparents' smallholding was a small house with several acres of land. There was no electricity and no gas, so we had oil lamps and coal fires. As there were no streetlights, you can imagine how dark it was in the winter when I came home from school at 4 o' clock.

There wasn't a bathroom, although we did have a flush toilet! The kitchen was referred to as the scullery and all the cooking was done either on a Primus stove in the scullery or on a large black cast iron range, which was in my grandparents' quarters. This was also where we ate all our meals.

My grandmother was a traditional, stoic, Protestant Scotswoman. Her embedded Presbyterianism meant that to her, the answer to all life's problems was simply to work harder! I remember she had many sayings mostly designed to make sure that you didn't get above your station. I can picture her now saying "it's a sair ficht for a half loaf son," which basically meant life is hard work: it's a sore fight and you only get half of what you want! I was the first grandchild and both grandparents looked after me very well and loved me very much, in their own way.

We lived simply. There were no shops nearby, so we bought our milk and meat directly from the farmer and what vegetables we didn't grow came from Willy Smart's farm. Once in a while there would be a trip into town on the tram to pick up supplies that we couldn't get locally. My grandma was a simple cook and all meals were basic. Things like meat and potatoes and broth were staples, which I really enjoyed but it was always exciting to see the clootie dumpling pot steaming away on the big black range in my grandparents' room. Cloot means cloth, so clootie dumpling is a rich dried fruit and suet pudding boiled in a cloth. Because it took a long time to cook it was a delicious treat reserved for high days and holidays, like birthdays or the New Year, when my grandmother would hide a thruppence in the pudding for one of us to find. I really hope you enjoy trying this recipe.

DAVID HARDMAN (AND HIS DAUGHTER ELIZA MORELAND)

CLOOTIE DUMPLING

Preparation time: 30 minutes • Cooking time: 2 hours 20 minutes • Serves 6

250g self-raising flour • 250g mixed dried fruit • 150g sugar • 75g grated suet (or vegetarian alternative) • 100g breadcrumbs • Pinch of salt • 1 tsp mixed spice • 1 tsp baking powder • 200ml milk • 2 tbsp black treacle • 2 tbsp golden syrup • 1 large egg, lightly beaten

Fill a large pan with water, not quite to the top (leave a 5cm gap and ensure there is enough room for the clootie dumpling to float) and bring it to the boil.

Combine all the dry ingredients – flour, dried fruit, sugar, suet, breadcrumbs, salt, mixed spice and baking powder – in a large mixing bowl.

In a second bowl, whisk together the milk, treacle and golden syrup. Add the egg once the mixture has cooled slightly and whisk again until thoroughly mixed. Pour the milk mixture into the dry ingredients and fold with a large metal spoon until it comes together into a doughy consistency: this is the dumpling!

For the next part, you will need to run a clean tea towel or thick muslin (the cloot!) under water and then wring it out before laying it flat and lightly dusting the entire surface with flour.

Shape the mixture into a dumpling and place in the centre of the cloth. Take each corner and bring together to wrap the dumpling up, tying the corners together or using string to secure.

Use a spoon to lower your dumpling into the pan of water, which should be simmering. Leave to boil for 2 hours with a lid on, checking often to make sure the water is always covering the dumpling and topping up when necessary.

Preheat the oven to 180°c (160°c fan or Gas Mark 4) and once the dumpling has boiled for 2 hours, take it out of the water and gently peel the cloth away. Put the clootie dumpling onto a baking tray and pop in the oven for 15 to 20 minutes until you see a skin has covered the surface of the pudding.

The clootie dumpling is done! Serve with a dollop of cream or hot custard.

SHARING OUR ...
CELEBRATIONS

"Whenever we would have guests, family and friends over, butter chicken would be the star of the show. A huge cauldron-sized serving dish in the middle of the table had people fighting over who gets to it first. Sitting around the table together as a family, enjoying the food and company, laughing and joking together, all bonding over our love for the food and each other are memories that I will hold close to my heart forever." – Ben Woolf

MY MUM'S FAMOUS BUTTER CHICKEN

How can I put this into such few words? Nothing reminds me more of my childhood than coming home to the aromas and scents of my amazing mum preparing her "famous butter chicken". The exact moment I smelled the sautéed onions, ginger and garlic alongside the creamy, buttery gravy, I knew right then and there exactly what we were having for dinner.

The first thought that would spring to mind would be to sneak into the kitchen and pour myself a quick bowl when Mum wasn't looking. However, the majority of the time I would get caught red-handed! But it was always followed by a smile and this response from Mum: "Here my darling, have as much as you want." She would remind me that Maharajas loved eating this too and how it is part of our Indian history. As easy as it sounds to savour all the different flavours, it's near impossible not to eat the whole bowl in a matter of minutes!

Whenever we would have guests, family and friends over, butter chicken would be the star of the show. A huge cauldron-sized serving dish in the middle of the table had people fighting over who gets to it first. Sitting around the table together as a family, enjoying the food and company, laughing and joking together, all bonding over our love for the food and each other are memories that I will hold close to my heart forever.

The preparation, commitment, love and planning that is involved in making such a simple yet mouth-watering dish never ever failed to amaze me. For someone like myself who has tried to learn many cooking tips and tricks from my mum, I can never seem to create something that comes close to the perfection of her cooking. Tender chicken pieces, with a perfectly balanced spicy yet creamy sauce accompanied by perfect, fluffy, fragrant rice. This complete meal warms your stomach and your heart with nothing but joy and great memories.

MY MUM'S FAMOUS BUTTER CHICKEN

This is best made by marinating the chicken overnight. Thigh meat is best, or you can use a mixture of breast and thigh if preferred.

Preparation time: 15 minutes, plus 12 hours marinating • Cooking time: 1 hour • Serves 4

For the marinated chicken • 2 large pieces of skinned chicken breast • 3 large boneless chicken thighs • 115ml full-fat Greek or unstrained yoghurt • 3 cloves of garlic, finely chopped • 2 Kashmiri chilies, roughly chopped • 2 green chillies, finely chopped, or 1 tsp chili powder • 2.5cm (1 inch) fresh ginger, peeled and finely chopped • 1 lemon, juiced • 2 tbsp tandoori masala • 1 tbsp each ground turmeric and coriander • 1 tbsp olive oil • 1 tsp salt

For the sauce • 85g butter • 5 tbsp olive oil • 1 medium onion, sliced • 2 tbsp tandoori masala • 1 tsp ground coriander • ½ tsp each ground turmeric and red chilli powder • 200g tomato passata • 2 tbsp tomato purée • 4 tbsp double cream • 150ml soured cream • 1 tsp dried fenugreek leaves • 100ml hot water • 100g baby spinach leaves • Small bunch of coriander leaves, roughly chopped

For the marinated chicken

Score the chicken breast and thighs deeply without cutting right through, then cut them into 2 or 3 inch chunks. Put the yoghurt in a large bowl and whisk so there are no lumps and it is a smooth pouring consistency. This will help the yoghurt not to separate when cooking. Add the remaining ingredients to the bowl and whisk again, then coat the cubed chicken in the marinade. Cover and leave in the fridge to marinate for at least 1 hour, but overnight is best for all the spices to meld.

When the chicken is marinated, heat up the grill as hot as it will go. Shake the excess marinade off each piece of chicken (keep the marinade for the sauce) and grill for 5 minutes on each side. The chicken should be part-cooked and should have a slightly charred colour. Set aside.

For the sauce

Heat up a wok or large pan with the butter and olive oil in. When hot, add the sliced onion and fry until soft and light brown. Stir in the spices and cook for another 2 minutes, then quickly add the passata and tomato purée. Cook the sauce on a medium heat for a further 3 to 4 minutes, then turn off the heat and leave it to cool.

Whisk the leftover marinade until smooth. When the sauce is cool, put the pan back on a very low heat and slowly pour in the marinade. Cook on this heat for 5 minutes, then pour in the soured and double cream. After 3 to 4 minutes, fold in the grilled chicken pieces. Sprinkle in the dried fenugreek leaves and mix it all together until it's coated in the sauce and then add the hot water. Bring to a slow boil and then turn down the heat to a simmer and semi-cover the pan with a lid. Continue cooking until you have a fairly thick sauce (this should take around 10 minutes). Add a little more water if you want a bit more sauce.

Stir in the spinach leaves and then as they wilt, scatter over the fresh coriander. Serve your butter chicken with plain basmati rice.

TO SAVITA, FROM KALPNA

With five hungry children and a gruelling full-time job, my mother still managed to make lovely food for us every day. At weekends, our home would fill up with friends and family and all of us sisters would help her in the kitchen, all trying to outshine each other and to impress our guests, but above all to give our mum the relief she deserved from cooking and looking after us all after a long week's work. Although we only ate meat on weekends (normally on a Saturday), we couldn't afford expensive foods, so we would try to make the vegetarian dishes which took a little longer or elevate our normal dishes. Each one of us cooked and we all cooked differently. My sister Savita's cooking was colourful and elegant, like her clothes, and always very creative. Outside the world was in flower-power, love and peace mode, and at home, Savita would draw flowers on our faces and braid wildflowers into our hair. We let our imaginations run free. I remember her making this pilau, full of neatly chopped delicious vegetables. We would adorn it with thin slices of boiled egg and fresh tomatoes in the shape of flowers and present it with a smile.

SAVITA'S SATURDAY NIGHT SPECIAL VEGETARIAN PILAU

Preparation time: 20 minutes • Cooking time: 40 minutes • Serves 4

10 tbsp oil • 2 tbsp cumin seeds • I large onion, sliced • 2.5cm (I inch) fresh ginger, grated • 4-5 bay leaves • 6-7 green cardamom pods, gently smashed to partially open • I tsp ground turmeric • I tsp red chilli powder • I tsp ground coriander • I tsp salt • 3 medium tomatoes, finely chopped • I large potato, diced • 8-10 green beans, chopped into small pieces • 7-8 small cauliflower florets • I red pepper, diced • 75g fresh or frozen peas • 250g basmati rice

To serve • 2 boiled eggs, thinly sliced • 2 small fresh tomatoes, sliced into thin rounds • 3-4 small green chillies, sliced lengthways (optional)

Heat the oil in a heavy-based large pan with a tight-fitting lid. Fry the cumin seeds and as they sizzle, add the onions. Cook for 2 to 3 minutes on a medium heat and then stir in the ginger, bay leaves and cardamom pods. Continue cooking until the onions are light brown, then mix in all the spices and half the salt. Cook for 2 minutes before stirring in the fresh chopped tomatoes. Cook for a further 3 to 4 minutes until the tomatoes are mashed. Add the diced potato, green beans and cauliflower florets. Cook for another 3 to 4 minutes until par-cooked and then mix in the red pepper and peas.

Measure the rice in a cup or jug so you know how much water to add. Wash the rice until the water runs clear and drain. Add the rice and remaining salt to the pan, then stir until the rice is coated with the spices. Quickly pour in twice the amount of hot water as rice and bring to the boil. Boil for 2 minutes and then reduce the heat to a simmer. Cover with a tight-fitting lid and leave to cook for 12 to 15 minutes until the rice is done and the water has evaporated. Do not stir the rice while it's cooking.

To serve

Arrange the rice, gently separating the grains, on a large flat plate and then decorate with the slices of boiled egg, tomato and green chilli if using.

YI ZENG

PEARL MEATBALLS

Preparation time: 20 minutes, plus 2 hours soaking • Cooking time: 20 minutes • Makes around 15

100g glutinous rice • 200g pork mince • 1 tbsp light soy sauce • 2 tsp sesame oil • ½ tsp salt

If you want me to choose one dish that represents my hometown, and has the most memories attached to it, I'd have to say pearl meatballs. This is basically steamed pork meatballs coated with glutinous rice. Because they are cooked in this special way, the meatballs are very juicy and tender, and the glutinous rice is soaked with meat juice, so you can taste the rich flavours without dipping them in any sauce.

The pearl meatball is a traditional dish in Hubei; we usually eat this when it is Chinese New Year or when friends and family come together. Because making this dish does not require a knife, my mom would allow me to be the second chef as a child, helping her to roll the meatballs in the glutinous rice to coat the whole surface. I really liked this game when I was young.

Now, I have settled in the UK. But every time I have friends visit me or when I miss home, I will cook this dish. It is really simple to make, but it is so delicious and brings back lots of lovely memories.

Soak the glutinous rice in water for 2 hours, making sure the water level is always above the rice.

In a large bowl, combine the pork mince, light soy sauce, sesame oil and salt. Mix everything well.

Drain the glutinous rice and then transfer it to a big plate. Scoop out about 1 tablespoon of the pork mixture and shape it into a ball.

Roll the meatball around the plate of glutinous rice until the surface is fully coated. Gently press the meatball to make sure the rice sticks to it. Repeat this process with all the pork mixture and rice.

Place the coated meatballs in a steamer, leaving at least 1cm of space around each one. Steam the pearl meatballs for 20 minutes, the final size will be slightly bigger than Swedish meatballs, then they are ready to serve.

We usually eat this as a main dish or like dim sum because it contains both meat and rice. It doesn't need a dipping sauce or anything else served with it.

TO KAVITA, FROM KALPNA

KAVITA'S PARTY JEERA CHICKEN WINGS WITH RED ONION RELISH

This isn't real jeera chicken without the freshly roasted cumin powder. It's easy to make; just roast the seeds in a dry pan on a low heat for 4 to 5 minutes until the aroma is released and then grind with a pestle and mortar. It makes this starter sing!

Preparation time: 10 minutes • Cooking time: 30 minutes • Serves 4

8 tbsp rapeseed oil • 3 tbsp cumin seeds • 1 large red onion, finely sliced • 1 tbsp grated fresh ginger • 3 cloves of garlic, minced • ½ large red chilli, finely chopped • 12-16 skinned chicken wings • 3 tbsp lemon juice (fresh or from a bottle) • 1 tbsp roasted and ground cumin seeds, plus 1 tsp for garnish • 1 tsp ground coriander • 1 tsp ground turmeric • 1 tsp paprika (unsmoked) • Salt, to taste • Fresh coriander leaves

For the red onion relish • 1 small red onion, very finely sliced • ½ small lemon, juiced • ¼ red chilli, finely chopped • Fresh mint leaves, chopped

Prepare the red onion relish first. In a bowl, cover the sliced onion in cold water and soak for 10 minutes. Drain off the water and pour over the lemon juice. Mix in the chopped chilli and mint, then leave the flavours to meld for 10 to 15 minutes while you cook the chicken wings.

In a wok-style pan, heat the oil to a medium temperature. Put in the cumin seeds, allow them to sizzle and then add the onion, ginger, garlic and red chilli. Cook until the onion is soft and then mix in the chicken wings to coat them with the aromatics.

Pour in the lemon juice and continue to cook while stirring for 5 minutes. Add the ground spices (cumin, coriander, turmeric and paprika) with some salt and then mix well. Cook for another 5 minutes on a medium heat. The spices should coat the chicken and the chicken should be browned.

Cover the pan, reduce the heat to a simmer and leave until the chicken wings are cooked through. If the chicken is sticking, add a few tablespoons of water.

Serve the jeera chicken wings on a flat dish, sprinkled with fresh coriander leaves and the extra roasted cumin, with the red onion relish on the side.

Jeera chicken wings remind me of the carefree days when all our family and friends would come together every weekend to eat, dance and celebrate. Bollywood dancing days: dressing up, bling and bhangra were obligatory as was the table laden with starters and snacks while the main courses bubbled away in the kitchen. The centrepiece starter, enjoyed by everyone from grandparents to grandchildren, was my sister Kavita's jeera chicken wings. Piled high on a plate, the jeera wings would be preceded by a delicious aroma of freshly roasted cumin seeds. The music would be cut, and everyone would move eagerly towards the table. This dish has multi-dimensional flavours on one plate and is perfect to re-energise a party before the slow move back to the dance floor. It was always party time in our home, and even now, as our dancing days slow down, these chicken wings continue to be made and we remember the happy times we shared together.

NASI KEBULI
THE ROYAL RICE

This Malaysian-style biryani is a chicken and rice dish originating from the Kuala Lipis district in my home state of Pahang, Malaysia. Legend has it that the dish was invented when the sultan of the state visited a local village and wanted to eat something with chicken. The cook, who was not expecting this surprise visit, quickly threw together chicken, rice and spices in a pot and served it as 'Nasi Kebuli' (a combination of the royal titles 'Kebawah' and 'Duli') to the sultan. It quickly became a royal favourite and to this day is still served during royal banquets and state dinners. What makes this dish special is the use of kaffir lime leaves and lemongrass which highlight the subtle flavour of the rice. You can also serve nasi kebuli with a Malaysian style sambal chilli or egg korma, but I have paired it with a simple yet punchy cucumber and pineapple salad.

Preparation time: 25 minutes • Cooking time: 1-2 hours • Serves 6

---

4 cups (approx. 700g) basmati rice • Salt • I large whole chicken • I tsp ground turmeric • 400g shallots • 80g fresh ginger • 30g galangal • 2 cloves of garlic • 4 lemongrass stalks, white part only • I tbsp coriander seeds • I tbsp black peppercorns • 2 litres water • 2 cups (approx. 450g) oil • 3 tbsp butter • 4-5 kaffir lime leaves • I pandan leaf, cut into 4cm pieces (optional) • For the salad • I cucumber • ½ pineapple • 2 medium onions • I red chilli • 3 tbsp sugar • 2 tbsp white vinegar • ½ tsp salt • For the broth (optional) • ½ onion, diced • I star anise • 3 cardamom pods • 3 cloves • I x 2.5cm cinnamon stick • I chicken stock cube

Photo: Mireya Gonzalez

First, wash the rice until the water runs clear, then soak it in fresh water with 4 tablespoons of salt for I hour. Meanwhile, clean the chicken and pat dry, then rub it with the turmeric and a teaspoon of salt.

Thinly slice the shallots, ginger, galangal and garlic. Bruise the lemongrass by bashing it gently and then put all the prepared ingredients into a large pot with the coriander seeds, peppercorns and water. Add the prepared chicken and top up with enough water to cover it completely. Bring to the boil, then cover and simmer until the chicken is cooked through. Remove the chicken from the broth and drain. Reserve the stock.

In a large wok, heat the oil and fry the chicken until golden all over. Either cut the chicken into pieces of your preferred size or leave it whole as is the traditional way of serving this in Malaysia. Cover the chicken with tin foil and keep warm in the oven.

Heat a quarter cup (approximately 55g) of the frying oil in a medium saucepan while you drain the soaked rice. Once hot, gently sauté the rice for 5 minutes. Add 3.5 cups (approximately 830ml) of the reserved chicken stock to the pan with a teaspoon of salt, the butter, lime leaves and pandan leaf if using. Stir until combined and bring to the boil before reducing the heat. Simmer with the lid on until the rice is cooked and all the liquid has been absorbed.

To serve the nasi kebuli, fluff the cooked rice with a fork, transfer it to a large platter and place the cooked chicken on top. Garnish the dish with lettuce, tomatoes and crispy shallots.

Just before serving the nasi kebuli, make the salad. Cube the cucumber and pineapple, thinly slice the onions and slice the chilli. Stir the sugar, vinegar and salt together until the sugar has dissolved. Mix the salad with the dressing and serve straight away.

If you have extra chicken stock left over, you can serve this as a broth on the side. Fry the onion in a tablespoon of oil until fragrant, then add the whole spices and fry again fragrant. Add the chicken stock, bring to the boil, then turn down the heat and let it simmer for 10 minutes. You can also add the stock cube to give the broth more flavour if needed. Garnish with crispy shallots and fresh coriander leaves, then serve with the nasi kebuli.

ASHER'S KWANZAA MACARONI CHEESE

I don't use any form of measurements to make my macaroni cheese; it's done by eye and taste and the number of people I plan on feeding. I use pasta twists, shells, bows or a mixture and for the cheese, a combination of extra strong cheddar, medium cheddar and red Leicester.

Preparation time: 20 minutes • Cooking time: 40 minutes • Serves 5-6

300g pasta • ½ a small red, yellow and green pepper • 1 onion • 1 clove of garlic • 2 tbsp butter • 2 tbsp crushed black peppercorns • 1 tsp all-purpose seasoning • 1 tsp dried mixed herbs • 4 heaped tbsp plain flour • 500ml milk • 250g grated cheese

Kwanzaa means a full house for me, and my macaroni cheese is a must. Kwanzaa is a week-long celebration from the 26th of December to the 1st of January which honours people of African heritage. Each day is dedicated to different principles to reflect on: umoja (unity), kujichagulia (self-determination), ujima (collective work and responsibility), ujamaa (cooperative economics), nia (purpose), kuumba (creativity) and imani (faith). On the 1st of January, we give each other presents and eat even more mac and cheese!

My macaroni cheese is made with lots of cheese, milk, seasoning and lots and lots of love. Everyone has their own special recipe, and no two people make it the same. This recipe is my own creation. It truly is a dish for the soul. My daughters and their friends have attempted to replicate my recipe; a few have come close but every time they say that there is nothing better than their mother's cooking. I'm sharing it here so my daughters always have this as a reminder of me, our wonderful feasts, family events and celebration days.

Put the pasta in a large pan of salted water to boil. Preheat the oven to 200°c (180°c fan or Gas Mark 6). Meanwhile, dice the peppers and finely chop the onion and garlic. Heat the butter in a large pan or wok, then sauté the vegetables.

Stir the peppercorns, seasoning and herbs into the vegetables, then start adding the plain flour 1 spoonful at a time. Stir in some of the milk to make a thick paste consistency. Keep stirring in the flour and milk to create a smooth sauce.

Add the grated cheese to the sauce and mix in the remaining milk. Make sure the cheese has melted and the consistency of the sauce is sufficient to cover the pasta.

Drain the cooked pasta and transfer it to a large baking tray or ovenproof glass dish. Pour in the cheese sauce, making sure the pasta is completely covered. If you have any grated cheese left, sprinkle it on top. Bake the macaroni cheese in the preheated oven for about 30 to 40 minutes. Voila!

KEEMA KOFTE

Our religions and countries may often be sadly divided, but our food histories are also often inextricably intertwined going back generations, sometimes centuries, and that's very much the case for my family and our favourite dishes which we grew up with.

My father was born and brought up in Sialkot and my mother in Multan, Indian towns which then became part of Pakistan during partition. Until then my Hindu families had lived cheek by jowl with their Muslim neighbours; they were schooled together, worked together and often feasted together. Even after partition when they fled to New Delhi as refugees, they still ate the foods which were rooted in their childhoods.

They were always proud of their connection to their birthplace and my father was proud that he read and wrote Urdu. He never forgot his connection to the place which is now Pakistan. The language, the friendships and the foods were always in his memories. Dad would often reminisce about the fertile fields full of ripe vegetables, gigantic watermelons, exotic fruits of every kind and succulent mangoes hanging from trees in the streets.

The dishes my family grew up with were steeped in historic richness going back centuries. The pervasive influence of herbs and spices in Indian cuisine originally goes back to the conquests of Alexander the Great in 325BC. India's art, music, poetry, food and language were hugely inspired by the Moghuls when they occupied Northern India. Historical records from the time reveal royal court kitchens overseen by hundreds of chefs producing sumptuous meals for daily consumption and accounts of feasts which outshone anywhere in the world.

The Moghuls loved indulgence and they were great writers, poets, musicians, artists and hunters. The pinnacle of this art and architecture starred in the Maharaja's palaces, rich textiles and one of the world's seven wonders, The Taj Mahal, the extraordinarily mesmerising marble mausoleum constructed by Emperor Shajahan for his beloved wife, Mumtaz.

The Moghul Emperor's kitchens trained Hindu chefs and so those dishes have become interwoven in our culture. To this day, we enjoy the complex spicy and creamy dishes jewelled with rich dried fruits, nuts and often adorned with gold and silver leaf.

All that extraordinary history is part of so many recipes from my family's past. They represent shared cultures, shared humanity: the unity and togetherness of the communities who lived harmoniously, no matter their religion, background or language. These recipes are still important to me and were cooked for special occasions. Keema Kofte is one such dish, rich and with great depth of flavour.

KEEMA KOFTE
A DISH RICH IN SHARED HISTORY

Keema Kofte are lamb meatballs are mixed with garlic, ginger and spices and cooked in a thick, lush, concentrated tarka (sauce). A dish enjoyed by kings and families alike, which is what my father used to say. Fresh mint will take some of the 'fatty' taste away from the lamb. To check the seasoning, I make a small kofte, cook it separately in a frying pan and taste it, then adjust accordingly. A wide-bottomed casserole dish is good for this recipe.

Preparation time: 30 minutes • Cooking time: 1 hour • Serves 4

For the kofte • 5 cloves of garlic • 2.5cm (1 inch) fresh ginger • 3 green chillies • 500g finely minced lamb • ½ tsp salt • ½ tsp red chilli powder • 1 tsp ground coriander • 1 tbsp oil • Small handful of fresh coriander stems, finely chopped • Fresh mint leaves, finely chopped

For the tarka • 8-10 tbsp oil • 2 cinnamon or cassia sticks • 1 medium onion, finely chopped • 1 tsp ground turmeric • 1 tsp ground coriander • 1½ tsp red chilli powder (according to taste) • ½ tsp garam masala • ½ tsp salt • 1 small tin of chopped tomatoes • 2 tbsp tomato purée • 3 tbsp hot water • Fresh coriander leaves

For the kofte

First, make a paste by combining the garlic, ginger and chillies with half a tablespoon of water in a blender. Put half of this paste into a large bowl and mix it with the minced lamb. Add the remaining ingredients, mix well, then leave the flavours to meld for 15 to 20 minutes while you make the tarka. You can also make the kofte in advance, then cover and refrigerate until needed.

For the tarka

In a large pan on a medium heat, heat the oil before frying the cinnamon sticks and chopped onion for 2 to 3 minutes. Stir in the remaining garlic, ginger and chilli paste. Cook until the onions are a medium brown colour, then add the spices and salt. After 2 to 3 minutes, pour in the chopped tomatoes, tomato purée and hot water. Reduce the heat to a simmer and cook until the sauce is smooth, around 8 minutes.

As the tarka is cooking, take small amounts of the minced lamb mixture and form into balls. When the tarka is ready, start to slowly add the koftes, taking care not to damage them. When they are all in, gently shake the pan and then cover with a lid. Leave to simmer for 5 minutes, then gently pour enough hot water to just cover the koftes into the tarka and bring to the boil. Leave to cook for 20 minutes until the kofte are done. Serve garnished with the coriander leaves on a bed of basmati rice.

MINNIE WOOLF'S CHOLENT

It's traditional to invite friends and family to lunch on the Sabbath. The story goes that Minnie would carry the pot of cholent to the dining table and say "shittaryn' (pour it in) as the delicious meal was turned out onto a large plate for everyone to see.

Preparation time: 30 minutes • Cooking time: 12-24 hours • Serves 8-10

8 tbsp oil • 3 large onions, chopped • 4 tins of butter beans, drained • 500g pearl barley, rinsed • 2.5kg beef shin, cut into long chunks • 8 large carrots, cut into large slanted chunks • 8 sticks of celery, cut into large slanted chunks • 6-8 large potatoes, halved • Salt and white pepper • Hot beef stock

For the puddings (dumplings) • 60g tomor vegetarian margarine • 300g self-raising flour • 2 onions, grated • 2 eggs, beaten

Minnie Woolf was my great-grandmother. She came from a tradition of sharing food common in Jewish culture. Cholent is a hearty one-pot dish cooked slowly on a very low heat the night before and usually shared at the Sabbath lunch. The dish is cooked in this way because according to Jewish law, there are strict rules relating to the Sabbath. It is forbidden to do any form of work throughout the whole Sabbath. It is a day of rest. There are 39 prohibitions, one of which is "burning" so it is forbidden to create or extinguish a flame, or even to lower or increase its volume.

In Minnie's time, like all the other women, she would prepare the dish and take it to the local baker to be cooked overnight. Each of the self-contained Jewish villages, called shtetels, had a baker. The baker's ovens remained permanently alight and so the cholent could be cooked here gently for around 12 hours.

The flourish in the cholent is a large dumpling (known as a pudding) nestled in the middle of the casserole, which softens and soaks up all the flavours of the slow-cooked beef and vegetables. Some people add more than one dumpling as it is a delicious part of the cholent.

This recipe has been handed down by Minnie to her son Morris, then to Morris's son Alan and his wife Ginette before it came to me (Ginette's daughter), and I am still cooking it today.

Heat the oil in a large pot with a tight-fitting lid. Fry the chopped onions and when soft, add the butter beans and pearl barley. Cook for 2 to 3 minutes, then take off the heat and start to layer the meat and the vegetables in the pot. Season each layer with salt and white pepper.

For the dumplings

In a food processor, mix the margarine into the flour until you have fine breadcrumbs. Tip this mixture out, then blend the grated onion and beaten egg in the food processor. Season with salt and pepper, put the breadcrumb mixture back into the processor and blend into a dough. Take out and roll into two balls, using a little extra flour if the dough is sticky.

Gently place the dumplings in the middle of the pot between the meat and veg, then pour in enough hot beef stock to cover everything. Bring to the boil, put the lid on the pot, cover the whole thing with tin foil and tuck the edges in to stop the steam escaping, then place in a preheated oven at 130°c fan. Leave it to cook for at least 12 to 24 hours. Every few hours, shake the pot and top up with hot water if needed. The consistency should be moist but not dry.

MY MUM'S ROAST TANDOORI CHICKEN

Three months after Mum died, it was really important that we observe her Christmas traditions. As part of a non-Christian, immigrant family, I found Christmas tense as a child. You built up a set of cards from classmates that went unreciprocated; your parents grumbled at having to buy gifts for teachers paid to educate us; presents were a waste of money. And Diwali was always referred to as "Indian Christmas".

But we had our traditions, and Mum made us observe them. From my uncle staying over then driving to his house to shower (and us waiting for him in order for the festivities to start) to my best friend, Junaid, coming over for the meal and games, and phoning my ba (grandmother) and bapuji (grandfather) to say to them in a problematic Indian accent: "Merry Christmas." The best tradition, though, was Mum's roast tandoori Christmas chicken. She made it once a year and it was, without fail, delicious.

On our wedding day, my wife and I were presented with a book of recipes crowdsourced from our families. Pride of place was the recipe for Mum's roast tandoori Christmas chicken, written in her handwriting. It's the item I'd run back into a burning house to rescue. There's something powerful about seeing her handwriting.

The year she died, I took the recipe back to our childhood home so we could prepare for Christmas. My sister, wife and I were going to make the roast tandoori Christmas chicken, and in that first taste my sister and I would be transported back to Mum's kitchen, with the sound of sizzling onions and popping mustard seeds, the smell of garlic and garam masala and ginger and coriander, and the familiar sight of Mum, standing with one flip-flopped foot resting on a bench, cutting potatoes into the palm of her hand with the blunt, serrated, black-handled knife she used to cut everything from onions and chicken to garlic and fruit. This would be our time machine. If the kitchen looked and sounded like the kitchen I grew up in, it would be like she was there with us.

The recipe listed the things we needed for the marinade: yoghurt, ginger and garlic, tomato purée, chilli powder, turmeric, ground cumin and coriander, garam masala, finely chopped fresh coriander and two serving spoons of oil. However, we didn't have any tomato purée, only four cherry tomatoes. My wife suggested we chop them up finely and add them in with sugar. I said no. We had to do this properly. After 15 minutes of argument, my sister called a truce by placing Mum's metal marinating bowl in front of us. "Now what?" she asked. "There's no measurements to go on."

I said: "We start with two serving spoons of oil."

"That's too much," said my wife.

"We stick to the recipe," I said firmly, pouring the oil over the chicken. My sister looked at the tray and poured in more oil. I glared at her. "It wasn't enough," she said. I added a pinch of all the spices and stirred.

"More salt," I said.

"There's no salt in the recipe."

"Mum put salt in everything," I told my wife. "We should put salt in."

"I thought you wanted to follow the recipe exactly," my wife said, flashing me a sarcastic smile. "We shouldn't put salt in if it doesn't say salt," my sister agreed.

We cut the chicken into pieces and rubbed the marinade over them, placing the trays in the fridge. It didn't feel right, I thought. There was too much oil. It was going to ruin the whole thing. That night I couldn't sleep, haunted by the excess of sunflower oil. I crept downstairs and as quietly as I could, pulled the trays of marinated chicken out of the fridge. The yoghurt marinade had separated from the extra unwarranted sunflower oil and there was a thick, greasy film swimming around the chicken. I poured the excess oil out, trying to stop the marinade disappearing with it.

Hours later, my sister and I sampled a piece of the cooked chicken before it was served. "Smells about right," I said. She nodded. "Every year Mum asked me if I wanted to learn how to make this," she said. "I don't know why I always said no."

"Mum's chicken smelled stronger than this, more chickeny."

I lifted the chicken to my mouth and put it in. There was a cacophony of tastes, the lilt of the lemon, ginger and garlic working like a tightly knit kabaddi team, the piquant persistence of the chilli powder, the warm gloop of yoghurt and the singe of cumin all dancing in my mouth, like a parade of elephants surrounded by bhangra dancers hoisting their arms in the air, with trumpets blaring and dhols banging. I rolled my head back in hypnotised, dizzying jubilation and … it didn't taste anything like my mum's roast tandoori Christmas chicken. It tasted like an imitation.

I swallowed the chicken and looked at my sister.

"It needs more salt," she said. And I agreed.

MY MUM JAYSHREE'S CHRISTMAS ROAST TANDOORI CHICKEN

We haven't given any measurements or timings here because there were none in the handwritten recipe that was handed down to us. It can serve however many people you need it to and be left to marinate overnight or for a few hours. As the story shows, perhaps it's all down to personal taste and so you can experiment with this marinade to find your own perfect balance of flavours.

---

1 free-range chicken • Yoghurt • Ginger • Garlic • Tomato purée • Chilli powder • Ground turmeric • Ground cumin and coriander • Garam masala • Fresh coriander, finely chopped • 2 serving spoons of oil

Cut the chicken into small pieces (about 12) and remove the skin. Make two gashes on each piece. Mix all the ingredients except the oil together and rub the mixture over the chicken, making sure it covers the gashes to allow more flavour into the meat. Line a roasting tray with tin foil and drizzle over some of the oil. Arrange all the chicken pieces in the marinade on the tray and drizzle over some more oil. Leave the chicken to marinate for a few hours, or overnight in the fridge. Cook the tray of marinated chicken in the oven, turning the pieces as required, until done to your liking.

PINKY LILANI

PINKY'S DUHAN SALMON TIKKA

Preparation time: 10 minutes, plus 15 minutes marinating • Cooking time: 15 minutes • Serves 4

2 cloves of garlic • 5cm (2 inches) fresh ginger • ½ lemon, juiced • 2 large green chillies, finely chopped • Small handful of fresh coriander, chopped • 1 tbsp ground coriander • Pinch of salt • 8-10 grinds of black pepper • 4 salmon fillets (480g) • 1 lump of charcoal • 4 tbsp hot oil

First, peel the garlic and ginger then make a paste by blending them with a few drops of water. Combine this paste with the lemon juice, finely chopped chilli, fresh and ground coriander, salt and pepper. Cut the salmon fillets into large chunks and rub them with the marinade until coated. Leave to marinate for 10 to 15 minutes.

Par-cook the marinated salmon on a hot plate (or in a flat frying pan) and then place it in a heatproof glass bowl with a lid. Heat the lump of charcoal on the hob until hot and white on all sides, then place it in a small heatproof bowl. Put this small bowl in the middle of the glass bowl. Pour the hot oil carefully over the hot charcoal and as it begins to smoke, cover the larger bowl with a tight-fitting lid and leave for 5 minutes so the smoke infuses the salmon.

Serve the smoky salmon tikka with salad, grilled vegetables, dill pilau or naan bread.

When we lived in Calcutta, my family were lucky enough to have cooks who made our meals. Our chef, Hassan, was only 22 years old when he came to live with us. He came from a lineage of famous cooks in Uttar Pradesh, and he quickly became known as the best in Calcutta. He made the best biryanis and so many other wonderful dishes; people loved to come and eat with us. A house full of people sharing food: those were the best of times! Every time he cooked a dish, it was always perfect, because he was a perfectionist! People would say that he had "taste in his fingers" and often ask if they could watch him cook but he was a very private cook; he would say that this is his profession.

I learnt to cook when I got married and I still try to recreate his dishes, especially this one using the 'duha' technique, where a piece of charcoal adds smokiness to the dish. This can be done with any meats, especially kebabs, and for a vegetarian version, cooking aubergine in this method is also delicious.

TRUNG'S BUN CHA HANOI

This is not only one of my favourite dishes, but it also reminds me so much of my time back in the 1990s when I went to university in Hanoi, the capital of Vietnam.

I was born in a little coastal town called Cua Ong, home to only a few hundred households of which a good portion were family members. There were no restaurants, bars or even streetlights. Just one road in and one road out, very quiet. All my cooking knowledge came out of my mother's kitchen. But at 17 I passed my national exam and went to university in Hanoi. It was incredible; beautiful old buildings lined the streets, people bustling about and my first time seeing thousands of motorbikes on the road, restaurants everywhere and streetlights. It was a totally different experience from my little town. Every day I'd cycle through the old quarter after studying and I became transfixed by the smells of people cooking on every street corner. Fragrant smoke filled the air and I wondered what they were cooking. That was my first time eating bun cha!

The dish is a combination of marinated barbecued pork belly, minced pork meatballs in sweet fish broth, fresh rice noodles, salad leaves and an array of herbs, along with some lime, chilli and garlic. The pork belly is marinated and then grilled until the skin crisps. The meatballs are made from minced pork, shallots, honey, spring onion, garlic, pepper and of course some fish sauce. It's served with noodles and a mixed leaf salad, which balances the dish. This is known as Ying and Yang, a method that dominates all Vietnamese dishes.

People will sit outside on small plastic stools to eat bun cha and watch Hanoi life going by. It's a perfect lunch meal to eat in hot weather. Even the former US President Barack Obama tried it when he visited Hanoi in 2018.

Just thinking about bun cha makes me miss Vietnam. But now that I'm living in Bristol, I cook it at least once a week! I'd love to introduce all Bristolians to it.

BUN CHA HANOI
FROM THE SAIGON KITCHEN

For easier and faster preparation, use a disposable barbecue for the pork belly, or you can cook it under the grill indoors. Traditionally, we keep the skin on the pork belly. When making the meatballs, choose the proportion of lean and fatty pork according to your preference.

Preparation time: 1 hour, plus marinating overnight • Cooking time: 30 minutes • Serves 4-6

For the pickles • 1 small green papaya • 2 carrots or kohlrabi • 2 tbsp each salt and sugar • 4 tbsp white vinegar

For the meatballs and grilled pork belly • 400g minced pork • 400g pork belly, sliced • 10 cloves of garlic • 6 small shallots • 2 spring onions • 2 fresh hot chillies (or chilli powder, to taste) • Knob of fresh ginger • 4 tbsp each fish sauce and cooking oil • 2 tbsp each sugar and honey • 1 tsp each black pepper and salt • 1 egg

For the broth • 50g sugar • 50ml each white vinegar and fish sauce • 2 cloves of garlic, peeled

To serve • Limes, halved • Fresh chillies and garlic, finely chopped • 400-600g fresh rice vermicelli • Mixed lettuce and salad leaves • Fresh herbs, to taste (coriander, Vietnamese basil, perilla leaves)

For the pickles

Thinly slice the papaya and carrots or kohlrabi. Soak them in a bowl of water with 1 tablespoon of the salt for at least 1 hour, then drain and cover with 300ml of fresh water. Stir in the remaining salt, sugar and vinegar before covering the bowl and leaving the vegetables to pickle for at least 5 hours, or overnight for best results.

For the meatballs and grilled pork belly

Put the minced pork and sliced pork belly into separate bowls. Mash the garlic to a paste and finely chop the shallots, onions, chillies and ginger. Add half of all the ingredients except the egg to each of the bowls. Mix the egg into the minced pork mixture only. Marinate for 2 hours or leave it overnight in the fridge.

Form the chilled meatball mixture into about 16 small patties (the size of ping pong balls but shaped like plump burgers). Cook them under the grill for about 15 minutes on each side until the top and bottom are dark golden brown. It will take 20 to 25 minutes to cook the marinated pork belly under the grill. Remember to turn it once or twice.

For the broth

Dissolve the sugar in 500ml of water, then add the vinegar and fish sauce. Simmer the broth on a low heat for about 15 minutes. If you like, add more water or sugar to dilute the flavour. Add the garlic cloves 5 minutes before the broth is ready.

To serve

Place the pickled carrot and papaya into your serving bowls. Add a healthy portion of the grilled pork belly and 4 meatballs to each bowl, then pour the hot broth over them. Each person can add a squeeze of lime juice and some finely chopped chilli and garlic to their bowl for extra flavour according to their preferences. Serve the bowls with 100g of fresh rice noodles per person and plenty of salad and herbs on the side.

How to eat bun cha

If you're wondering how to eat bun cha, it's easy: just add some of the bun noodles, salad leaves and herbs to the bowl of broth so you can eat everything together. Keep adding noodles and greens as you eat; you don't need to put them all in at once. And of course, it's best eaten with chopsticks!

ESME DAVIS

In Guyana, it is the custom to eat 'cook up rice' on Old Year's Night (December 31st). This one pot dish is a combination of meat, beans and vegetables cooked in coconut milk with herbs and spices. It lasts all night, making sure the new year does not greet you without food.

GUYANESE COOK UP RICE

Preparation time: 25 minutes, plus 1 hour to marinate • Cooking time: 45 minutes • Serves 4

1kg skinless and boneless chicken thighs • 1 tbsp all-purpose seasoning • 2 tsp garlic powder • 2 tbsp dark soy sauce • 1 tbsp vegetable oil • 1 onion, diced • 500g butternut squash, diced • 4 carrots, diced • 4 spring onions, chopped • 2 tins of black-eyed peas • 2 tins of coconut milk • 1 tin of callaloo • 2 stock cubes • 2 tsp dried thyme • 1 scotch bonnet pepper (optional) • 1kg rice, washed • Salt and pepper, to taste • Fresh basil leaves, chopped

Wash the chicken, shake off the excess water and then coat in the all-purpose seasoning, garlic powder and soy sauce. Leave to marinate for 1 hour.

Heat the oil in a large pot, then add the marinated chicken thighs and diced onion. Fry while stirring occasionally until they get some colour. This takes about 10 minutes.

Add the squash, carrots, spring onions, black-eyed peas, coconut milk (along with a little water to rinse out the tins) and callaloo to the pan. Crumble in the stock cubes and dried thyme, then drop in the scotch bonnet if using: this is just for flavour so should be left whole and unbroken.

Bring the liquid in the pan to the boil, add the washed rice, stir and then bring back to the boil. Turn the heat down, cover the pan and simmer for about 10 minutes. Stir from the bottom during this time to prevent anything sticking.

After 10 minutes, add a little more liquid if needed, then cover and let it steam until the rice is cooked. Stir in the salt, pepper and chopped basil, cover again and leave for 5 minutes.

Serve the cook up rice with a side of sliced cucumber tossed in lime juice with a pinch of salt and hot pepper sauce.

MARTI'S PORTLAND JERK MARINADE

Growing up in England, jerk was not something that my family would cook but my dad, whose family is from Portland in Jamaica, would often talk about travelling to Boston Beach in Portland and being treated to jerk pork from the stalls there and it being cooked by his family as a feast after hunting wild boar in the 'bush' back home. My dad would tell us that jerk pork was something that we would try when we went to Portland. He said we were allowed to eat it as we were, like him, descended from the Maroons who had invented it.

The Maroons were originally hunters of wild boar. They were escaped slaves who lived in the hinterland of Jamaica and fought off the British for decades. They built escape routes from plantations across Jamaica and shuttled enslaved people to freedom, as well as leading numerous insurrections in their fight for freedom. They invented jerk as a method of cooking underground in pits which meant that there was no smoke so their hideouts could not be seen by the British. My dad is fiercely proud of his Maroon heritage.

The first time I had jerk was when I went to Jamaica as a teenager. It was at the end of my first whole day there and we had gone out in Spanish Town with my uncle. On the way back he said we would stop at his favourite jerk pit. I remember we all stopped at this pretty scruffy looking shack which was at the side of the road. Whole pigs were being cooked in a pit over wood and were covered by zinc panels. The ordering system was simple; you either asked for a quarter pound, half pound or more of meat. I ordered a quarter pound, which was my first mistake as it was not enough. A piece of the pig was lopped off, chopped up and handed to me in some foil with a couple pieces of bread and I was shown where the hot sauces were. It all happened really quickly but I do remember my uncle ordering his and saying 'mek sure yuh gi me de fatty piece of the meat'. I put some hot sauce on mine and put a piece of the meat in my mouth. It was amazing; I was instantly hooked by the smoky, spicy and sweet taste of it.

I'd had barbecue before, but this was something else. Jerk combined the flavours of the food that I had been brought up on (scotch bonnet, ginger, thyme, pimento) with the smoky taste of the wood. The atmosphere surrounding the jerk pit, with the noise of the people, the roar of the cars, the music blaring and the sensational taste of the meat, made this a spiritual experience for me. I instantly felt like I had arrived home.

I spent the rest of that holiday searching out more jerk pits. I also remember how miffed my dad was that, in the 20 years since he left Jamaica, jerk had gone from being something that was exclusive to his beloved Portland to being the street food of choice for all Jamaicans. An even more mobile version of cooking it had been invented by cooking it in halved steel pans, and you could pretty much get 'pan jerk' on every street corner.

We did go to Portland on that trip and had jerk pork made using wild boar at the famous Boston Beach. It was fantastic, so I did get a sense of what it was like for him. Then my dad, his brothers and some male cousins all left early one morning to go and get a wild boar so we could have a feast like the ones my dad had talked about, but they came back about four hours later a bit tipsy but with a wild ram goat and not a boar. So unfortunately, I did not see them build the pit they boasted about, although the ram goat was really tasty!

MARTI'S PORTLAND JERK MARINADE

My dad's sister taught me how to make this marinade. She lives on the most beautiful smallholding up in the Portland hills; you can see Cuba across the ocean from her terrace and most of the ingredients can be found on her land. The only change I made is using white wine vinegar and lime juice instead of ordinary vinegar.

Preparation time: 10 minutes, plus 12-24 hours marinating • Makes enough to fill a 500ml jar

---

75g brown sugar • 50g spring onion • 40g scotch bonnet chillies • 30g thyme leaves • 25g fresh garlic • 25g fresh ginger • 25ml molasses • 20g allspice • 15ml lime juice • 15ml white wine vinegar • 5g salt • 2.5g cinnamon • 2.5g ground cloves • 1.25g nutmeg • 1.25g freshly ground black pepper

So how do you make the dish of jerk pork, chicken or even fish? For the marinade, simply measure out the ingredients and then blitz all of them together in a food processor or liquidiser. We use a Thermomix as I like my marinade to be really smooth. Once that's ready, you just marinate some meat or fish in it. I like pork but also use chicken occasionally. The marinade can be used, and is also delicious, with most other meats, fish and tofu. I have even had it with halloumi on a barbecue.

Ideally, the meat would be cooked in a jerk pit using pimento wood and covered with zinc, which has the effect of roasting, steaming and grilling the meat all at once. This is what makes it so special when you have it in Jamaica. However, most of us do not have a jerk pit so generally just grill the marinated ingredient slowly on the barbecue. It can also be roasted or grilled indoors but again, if grilling, make sure to do it slowly.

To accompany your jerk dish, you can go down the traditional route and have it with hot sauce and bread or make rice and peas. I usually do a plantain salad, sweet potatoes, roasted yam and pickled red cabbage.

This marinade is not something you would make just for one round of jerk. I generally spend a whole day, usually in the spring, making enough marinade (using 25 times the quantities of the ingredients above) for the whole summer and enough so that I can give away a few jars to my family and friends.

The major family-orientated holidays in the United States, where I grew up, are Thanksgiving and Christmas. On these occasions, my parents would host all the relatives that lived nearby for a lunchtime celebration that we looked forward to for months in advance. These relatives included my maternal grandmother and her widowed sister, another great aunt and great uncle, and possibly my paternal grandmother. Our house was large enough to also include relatives who may have travelled from outside our state to visit us at this joyous time. Our out-of-state guests generally included cousins roughly the same age as my sister and me as well as their parents, so our house was full of young people, elders, laughter and fun.

Preparations for the meal usually began the night before. My maternal grandmother, who lived with us, tended to do much of the cooking for occasions large and small. Sometimes, I would help her with the cutting and chopping the night before the big lunchtime gatherings. Mother would bake a cake for dessert and my treat was to lick the last of the cake batter from the spoon after it was poured into the tins for baking. Dad performed the ceremonial cracking of the coconut as his contribution to the meal.

The banquet was sumptuous by our modest standards. A lace tablecloth covered the dining room table, which was laid with my mother's best china, silver cutlery and beautiful glassware. Our dining room looked spectacular with silver candle holders holding tall white tapers and chairs brought from the kitchen to accommodate everyone.

We always started the meal with my mother's ambrosia, a fruit salad containing fresh grapefruit and freshly grated coconut. A large turkey formed the centrepiece and among the many vegetable dishes was the savoury sweet potato bake recipe I've shared here. The dish can be seasoned to suit your individual tastes, with more or less vegetables, salt and sugar as you wish.

THANKSGIVING SAVOURY SWEET POTATO BAKE

Preparation time: 30 minutes • Cooking time: 1 hour • Serves 4

4 tbsp butter • 2 medium onions, diced • 3 sticks of celery, finely chopped • 2 medium sweet potatoes, finely diced • ½ a medium butternut squash, finely diced • 4 carrots, diced • 2 handfuls of chopped pecans • Salt, to taste • 1 unpeeled orange, sliced • 2 tsp sugar • Ground cinnamon

Melt the butter in a large, heavy saucepan and add the onions and celery. Cook slowly for 10 minutes. Add the sweet potatoes, butternut squash and carrots. Cook slowly with the lid on the pan until soft, stirring occasionally. The vegetables should be tender enough to be mashed using a fork or potato masher. Add the chopped pecans and season to taste. In principle, add only a dash of salt.

Pour the mixture into an ovenproof dish and cover the entire surface with slices of orange. Sprinkle the sugar and a little ground cinnamon lightly on top of the orange slices. Bake in a preheated oven at 180°c for 30 minutes, then it's ready to serve.

SOPHIE COLE

My grandmother was a very good cook. Before our family moved to Hong Kong, all my food memories are in Dorset, where my grandmother cooked every meal (including bringing out a tea trolley of sandwiches and cakes, every single day). Her cooking style was, I suppose, traditional British food, and some of it was very time consuming. Thinking back, I can hardly imagine her anywhere other than in the kitchen, which is hardly surprising when, on top of the four meals a day she produced, she also made her own clotted cream, and it wasn't unusual to see a pig's head ready to make brawn, or a whole tongue being pressed.

Having lived through two wars, my grandmother's desire to make the most of every part of an animal was second nature to her, and she hated waste. She was in the fortunate position of having a gardener (in fact the same man, Ted, who was a gardener's boy in the same garden when she was growing up), and he used to leave fresh produce on the back steps for her every day from the huge range of vegetables and fruit that were growing there.

Christmas is the time in most households when you'd expect more cooking activity, and even my grandfather would do his bit, making crystallised apricots and pineapple pieces that he'd put in layers in a round wooden box that was only used once a year. My grandmother would make the Christmas cake at least six weeks in advance, and the Christmas pudding well before that. It's the Christmas pudding that has become my own contribution to the family Christmas.

My grandmother's handwritten cookbook (which has her name written in the front, and the year 1910) has all the food I remember so well from my childhood: Easter biscuits, coffee and walnut cake, brandy snaps, cold meat curry (with the then obligatory fruit, in this case an apple!), cottage pie, junket, and much more. In the early recipes, the cost of each ingredient is listed too. A cottage pie, for example, cost a grand total of one shilling and sixpence. It also included this family Christmas cake recipe.

MY GRANDMOTHER'S CHRISTMAS CAKE

Preparation time: 40 minutes
• Cooking time: 2 hours 15 minutes • Serves 10

228g plain flour • Pinch of salt • ½ tsp ground cinnamon • ½ tsp grated nutmeg • 170g butter • ½ a lemon or orange, zested • 170g dark brown sugar • 4 eggs, beaten • 454g sultanas • 340g seeded raisins • 228g glacé cherries • 114g almonds, blanched and shredded • 57g candied peel, shredded • 2 tbsp brandy, rum or sherry (or 1 tbsp orange juice) plus 1-2 tbsp for each week to 'feed' the cake

Prepare a 20cm (8 inch) cake tin by lining it with a double layer of greaseproof paper. Preheat the oven to 180°c or 160°c fan. Sift the flour, salt and spices into one bowl.

In another bowl, beat the butter until softened, add the lemon or orange zest and sugar, then continue beating until very soft. Add the eggs one at a time, beating between each addition.

Put the sultanas, raisins, cherries, almonds and candied peel into a third bowl. Add a third of the flour mixture and mix well. Use a metal spoon to fold the remaining flour into the butter mixture, and then fold the flour and fruit mixture into that, so everything is combined.

Mix in the spirit, sherry or fruit juice. Turn the mixture into the prepared cake tin and smooth out the top. Dip your fingers in warm water and dampen the surface slightly.

Bake the cake on the middle shelf of the preheated oven for 2 hours 15 minutes. After 1 hour, reduce the temperature to 165°c and cover the top of the cake with a double layer of greaseproof paper. After 2 hours, test the cake with a thin skewer – if it comes out clean, the cake is done – and remove from the oven or continue cooking accordingly.

Allow the cake to cool for 30 minutes in the tin, then turn out and leave to cool completely. Wrap the cake in greaseproof paper or foil and store in an airtight container. Feed it with 1 or 2 tablespoons of the alcohol you used in the mixture every week until icing. Do not ice the cake more than 1 week before Christmas.

HANNAH WYLIE

Growing up, family dinners were always an important event for us. Myself and my three siblings – Harriet, Katherine and Tom – all love to cook and have been doing so since we were little. Our mum Donna was a huge inspiration; she was making exciting, exotic food for a small Northamptonshire village in the late 90s. Mum was in turn inspired by her own mother, my Nana Kim, who was also breaking culinary boundaries in suburban settings: spaghetti Bolognese in Warwickshire in the 60s was pretty ground-breaking for an English family!

This recipe is my favourite dish that my nana used to make for us, a staple at Christmas and any other occasion we could use as an excuse. Nana Kim's trifle was notoriously boozy, but you can swap out the sherry for fruit syrup to make an alcohol-free version. It is simple, indulgent and delicious and it always makes me think of my family. I am quite partial to having leftovers for breakfast the next day, but I appreciate that may not be for everyone!

WYLIE FAMILY SHERRY TRIFLE

If fresh berries are not in season, defrosted ones work brilliantly for this trifle. We use Bird's custard powder, but you can make the custard from scratch if you prefer.

Preparation time: 20 minutes • Cooking time: 5 minutes • Serves 6

220g lady finger (savoiardi) biscuits • 75-100ml Bristol cream sherry or fruit syrup • 300g soft summer fruits, such as strawberries and raspberries • 570ml (1 pint) Bird's custard • 400ml double cream

In a large mixing bowl or trifle bowl, break up and layer the biscuits at the bottom of the bowl. Pour over the sherry or fruit syrup, aiming to cover the biscuits evenly. Leave for a couple of minutes so the biscuits can absorb the liquid and then mush gently with a fork.

Chop up the fruit roughly and add it to the bowl along with all the juice (or just pour the whole bag of defrosted fruit in).

Make the custard according to the instructions or your chosen method and then pour it over the fruit once at room temperature.

Whisk the double cream with a handheld or electric whisk until it forms soft peaks and then layer this on top of the custard.

Serve the trifle straight away or leave in the fridge until you are ready for it.

Photo: Rob Wicks @EatPictures

Photo: @JonCraig_Photos

Photo: Jim Lampard

Photo: Rob Wicks @EatPictures

Photo: Rob Wicks @EatPic

@JonCraig_Photos

Photo: @JonCraig_Photos

Photo: @JonCraig_Photos

Photo: @JonCraig_Photos

Photo: @JonCraig_Photos

ireya González

Thanks and Acknowledgements

Eat, Share, Love – this book has been a personal passion of mine for many years. From my childhood where sharing food with others was always at the heart of our daily family life, I have always understood that food and what it means to us can build bridges and make surprising new connections between all of us.

We have been gathering and curating these recipes for almost seven years and I am eternally grateful to all the contributors in this book who have given us their recipes and opened up their lives and hearts to me and to 91 Ways. Many of you have gone beyond kindness to help make this book happen including cooking lots of food and encouraging others to come forward and be part of the book too. It has been a privilege and an honour to hear your stories and to share a table with you.

I'm always grateful for all of my family's support, especially my sisters who not only shared their hearts, their personal memories and stories, but also emptied their wardrobes and homes to share their colourful clothes, textiles and decorations for the photoshoots; my darling Mark for being my everyday support and for giving me confidence in myself; and my precious son Ben who has become a passionate and brilliant cook in his own right and is now giving our family recipes and stories a new lease of life.

So many people have helped to bring this book together and given me encouragement and support. Special thanks to Breaking Bread, Team Canteen, Bianchis, John Manley, Moh, Christien, Maria Perez, and Hannah Boatfield, who all helped at key moments during the creation of this book; to my strong women role models Pinky Lilani, Kim Ingleby, and Xanthe Clay who have led the way in everything they do and always inspire me with their encouragement and backing; and to the support from Fiona Smith and the Meze Publishing team.

Over the years, many incredible and wonderful people have joined Team 91 Ways and worked hard to make it a success- you have been at the heart of 91 Ways, keeping me going with your passion, hard work and humour and all of our wonderful volunteers – we couldn't have run our events and made the much-needed connections without you and our wonderful ambassadors – always speaking up for 91 Ways and finding time to support us; our team of trustees – Sam, Jane, Adrian, Natasha and Marti – always offering wise counsel; and Total Produce for their enduring support. In the background, Sarah and Justine. You have all helped 91 Ways to make a real difference.

For many years, we have had the support of The National Lottery Community Fund and we would like to thank them wholeheartedly.

Finally, I'd like to pay tribute to my father and mother who came to this country full of hope, somehow overcame all the obstacles in front of them and showed me that the simple act of offering a plate of food to another can make a lasting and genuine connection and overcome divisions.